This book is dedicated to the amazing young adults out there! Whether you are in the workplace, university, high school or you, this is for you! I think you are smart and immensely inspiring! I love that you do your own thing, wear your own style and demand respect, truth, peace and equality! You are changing our world for the better!

You, the game changers, will demand that we get our act together with balanced eating! You will stand up and be heard and it will change everything!!!

I just know it!

Table of Contents

Red:	Soft or Hard Shell Tacos with Toppings
Yellow:	Chicken Caesar Pasta with Peas
Yellow:	Tomapplesauce Meatballs with Rice and Broccoli
Green:	Crunchy Orange Chicken with Potatoes and Spinach Salad
Green:	Tuna Tetrazzini with Corn & Peas

Table of Contents

Table of Contents

They Won't Cook or...
You're Too Scared To Let Them!

There's a quiet thing eating our mother's alive! They are sick about not having a healthy dinner with their families each night!

I arrive at the family's home. They are about to be interviewed to be on my show, *Fixing Dinner*, on The Food Network. They are shocked, excited and nervous that I have shown up for the interview (they imagined it would be a member of my crew)!

As mom tears off to put on lipstick (squealing something like, "I didn't do my haaaaaair!) I introduce myself to her enthusiastic young adults! They share that they are worried about mom. They admire how hard she works, but they know she is stressed... and that stresses them right out! I ask them if they help out with the cooking. They admit they don't do much! In turn, they say that mom either buys stuff that's easy for them to throw together or they love the food that she makes! I ask if they think they should know how to cook. **I mean really cook!** They all think it's very important for their own health and for the sanity of the household! Not only are they willing to be a part of that change, they are excited!!!

Before I finish telling you what happened next... I need parents and young adults to understand that the story I'm telling you isn't unique, it has become   the new normal! The parent or main cook of the family feels guilty asking his or her busy young adults for help. The parents don't ask because the parent feels it's something they should be doing FOR their kids! The parent's *guilt* means they don't want to pile extra work on their kids who are overwhelmed with activities and schoolwork. It's a story our parents convince themselves out of love! As a result it has created a society who chooses time over health over and over again. This is a truth we share with teens at the schools we visit!

Sooo, back to the story…Mom returns and apologizes once again for her appearance (which by the way is a heck of a lot better than mine). The conversation begins again, but with mom included. She tells me she watches the family's salt content and neeeeever uses anything with sugar. She barely uses take-out and hardly ever buys processed food!

Guess what happened next...

They Won't Cook or
You're Too Scared to Let Them!

I ask the mom why she's applied to be on the show if she's doing so well! She tells me she's a single mother and would like more variety and could really use some tips to make her tasks more doable!

...then comes the pantry sweep!

I ask to have a look in the pantry, freezer and fridge. I explain it's necessary for me to create a meal plan that's right for them! Mom's face turns eight shades of red as the freezer door opens and boxes and bags of processed burgers, meals, appetisers and pizzas spill out! Her gaze reveals her shock and that she has no idea where all that came from! The kids call her on it! She cries, I hug… and tell her she's not alone. Now... I can help!

So, here's the deal… My work has proven again and again that **time** and **guilt** is what's keeping North Americans unhealthy, not food! The food we eat is simply a symptom!

The healthiest relationships are those that encourage the ones you love, to be inspired and independent. Sometimes, for a variety of reasons, we hang on tight to being "the specialist" because it's easier to maintain the status quo! The mom in my story could be any parent! She wanted to appear perfect to her children, but in reality she wasn't coping very well at all and the kids knew it!

Cooking Together/Apart™

The goal of this book is to teach young adults and their families that cooking together is the solution to get dinner on the table, even if your prepping or cooking at different times. We have chosen the **Best and Easiest** meals, the ones families have raved about over the years. We've added watermarks for those who are Cooking Together/Apart (ignore them if you aren't). Our new "At A Glance" sticky note above the clock will help the Head Chef, whoever that happens to be, delegate tasks easily - even while rushing out the door for work!

I believe passing the torch to our amazing younger generation will allow them to change everything for the better! More importantly, they will get to experience what it was like way back when people worked together to accomplish the daily tasks in the home! Even if the new way is Cooking Together/Apart!

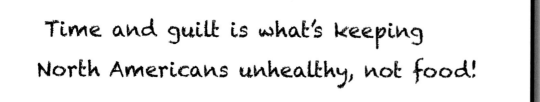

Time and guilt is what's keeping
North Americans unhealthy, not food!

Cooking Together/Apart™

A new easy way to get dinner on the table!

Cooking Together/Apart simply means that if a person can't get help from another person at the same time, or if they can't do it all at the same time, then they get help at a different time! This is not only easy to do in every situation, but it is literally life changing!

If you can relate to a situation below then you can use Cooking Together/Apart. Some situations may be a little trickier, but once you get the hang of it, you will never go back to the old way! In every single case, Cooking Together/Apart will help you to eat healthier, save a ton on groceries and save you swacks of time, all the while removing the, "What's for Dinner?" mind chatter in your busy work week.

Your typical work week. Can you relate to one of these scenarios?

- One parent gets home before the other.
- A teen, preteen or college student gets home before a parent.
- One roommate gets home before the other.
- A person works shifts, so starts work later than a partner, preteen, teen or college student.
- A single parent has babies, toddlers or young children.
- You live independently and have a dog or a cat, (and they are useless when it comes to cooking! Especially fish… they don't even fetch or cuddle). Sorry, I just couldn't stop!

On the following page, I'll show you how to adapt Cooking Together/Apart to your everyday life! But, before I do, we need to address the number one complaint of the main cook/shopper - What should I make for dinner? That's right! There are chapters written on it! It's joke material for comedians and it's every busy person's Achille's heel. If you really, really want to feel better about life in general, get everyone around you involved in picking five dinners for the upcoming week. Sound dumb or tooo simple? This step can take hours of stress out of your work week!

> Cooking Together/Apart™ will help you to eat healthier, save a ton on groceries and save you swacks of time all the while removing the, "What's for Dinner?" mind chatter in the work week! It's the ultimate in taking dinner off your mind!

If you're creating an Eat Sheet™ using a combination of your recipes and ours, then use the blanks at the back of the book or go to sandirichard.com and print a blank copy. If you're using meals from any of our books, our ESG™ (grocery list generator) will help you create your grocery lists in a flash!

Cooking Together/Apart™
How to Eliminate the "There's Nothing To Eat Syndrome!"

The Back-Up Plan is to ALWAYS leave your meal recipe out on the counter.

I will refer to this in the future as The Back-Up Plan. Now we're ready!

#1. One parent gets home before the other: Start cutting and chopping (check out the prep crew sticky note and water marks on the next pages) …buuuuut there's a sport or activity and you need to run out before you finish… HA! Leave the meal recipe out aka Back-Up Plan! The other parent will have everything right in front of them and really appreciate you for getting things started.

#2. One preteen, teen or college student gets home before a parent: Parents, if you are nervous that these brilliant individuals can't use knives or use a stove or oven, then take five minutes to cut things up the night before. Then leave the meal recipe out and someone else is in charge of assembly. Once a week do it together so that you can become more confident with their skill. Because believe me *their* confidence is probably not the issue!

#3. One roommate gets home before the other:
Refer to #1. Use the Back-Up Plan if something comes up.

#4. A person works shifts, so starts work later than a partner, preteen, teen or college student: Refer to example #1. Other family members: remember to serve out the shift worker's plate before your own. Set it aside in the fridge and then everyone else can serve themselves. That way the shift worker can eat and be freed up to do their part for the following day.

#5. A single parent has babies, toddlers or young children: Right after your kids go to bed or are playing, take a look at the meal for the next evening. Do just five minutes worth of cutting and chopping and have it in containers in the fridge. You will feel like 10,000 pounds has been lifted from your shoulders the next day! Make a note of another rule I'm famous for. If you have toddlers, make and serve the veggie first while you're making the rest of the meal. Kids will eat more veggies when they're hungry!

#6. You live independently: Refer to #5…Ignore the part when the kids are in bed or playing…and don't get the dog to help, that's just gross! LOL

Cooking Together/Apart ™
My Six Essentials for Dinner Success!

#1. Get 'em to pick 'em: Remember, when everyone gets to choose, everyone feels like they've been heard! Once they pick, they own that meal!

#2. This chef's specialty is: Daniel's famous Crunchy Orange Chicken with Potatoes and Salad. Mom's famous French Loaf Lasagna. Ownership goes a long way to having each person feel they are accepted for their choice. It also keeps people on track for who is doing what, when!

This week:
crunchy Orange chicken - Daniel
French Loaf Lasagna - Mom
Dijon Baked chicken - Zach!
Cheeseburger Soup! - Josh
Chicken Parmesan - Elissa

Dad, can you put the meat in the slowcooker the night before for me?

Thanks, Josh!

#3. Practice, practice, practice: If you are a beginner cook, don't move on to too many new meals at once. Wait until you've mastered the first couple (whether you are a young or old beginner). The goal in the workweek is speed. Once you know how to make a meal or two instinctively, it makes everything easier. You'll know when you want to try a new one. Don't be discouraged if it takes you longer at first... you'll get there!

#4. Reverse delegation: Mom, can you please remember to take my chicken out while I'm at basketball? Josh, I'm at study hall can you do the cutting so I can throw it together when I get back at 7:00 P.M? In the case of a family it's likely that Mom or Dad are going to pick up the groceries. But after that, everyone is busy. Sooo... little reminders really help!

#5. Don't worry about repeating favorites: Most people are uninspired with cooking dinner because they repeat the same 5-6 meals. If you are a family of 1, 2, 3, 4 or more and each is mastering a new dish or two, dinner is about to get really fun! Let it ease into it's own rhythm. When workweek dinner making seems peaceful, gradually add something new.

#6. Be considerate: Dad, what is your schedule like this week? Are you able to do Thursday? Ok, I can do Wednesday! Don't pick meatloaf on a day you are showing up at 7:30 P.M, unless you're able to get it ready the night before. Someone else can then pop it in for you so it's ready when you arrive! In other words, you are Cooking Together/Apart.

Monday — Crunchy Orange Chicken
Tuesday — French Loaf Lasagna
Wednesday — Dijon Baked Chicken
Thursday — Lean Mean Sheppard's Pie
Friday — Honey-Garlic Ribs

NO!

Make your meals and your schedules fit each other. Our meals are not laid out Monday to Friday. They are simply in groups of 5.

Your workweek may be Tuesday to Saturday. Only you know what your evenings look like. Soooo, match the meal type and speed with the chaos or calm in your unique schedule of a particular evening!

For super easy grocery shopping use our ESG™ (Grocery List Generator). Everyone can pick a picture of a meal they want from any book and with a click of a button, it will make your grocery list for you. Go to sandirichard.com and click on the Grocery List Generator tab in the menu bar.

What are the Watermarks? Use 'em or Don't!

You will notice in this book, we use a very faint watermark throughout the meal recipe. The watermark is placed directly over the instruction where there is cutting or chopping required or it's placed directly over the instruction where you use a stove-top or oven. We did this because behind every fabulous parent of a young adult, there's a young adult who probably doesn't know how to cook! (And when I say cook I'm not talking about throwing boxed food on a cookie sheet or in a microwave ooor making a sandwich)! If your family is the exception, the watermarks and sticky notes will just make your job even easier!

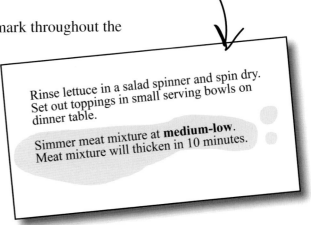

Rinse lettuce in a salad spinner and spin dry. Set out toppings in small serving bowls on dinner table.

Simmer meat mixture at **medium-low**. Meat mixture will thicken in 10 minutes.

When we sent the meals off to our test families this time around, their job was a little harder than usual. Not only did they need to test the meals that were updated for a better nutritional outcome or better cooking success; they also had to allow their 10-20 year old inexperienced cook make the meal. As we've come to expect, their comments were invaluable (once again hats off to our fearless and brutally honest test families)!

Aaaand here's what happened: The test families either loved the watermarks and raved about how helpful they are, or said they didn't pay much attention to them and in fact really didn't even notice them! Both of these responses were music to my ears! We purposely created the watermarks to be very faint so that you can either notice them or overlook them. Some of our families loved them and others didn't find them necessary. It depended on the age or cooking skill of their young adult. However, most families loved the sticky notes for that extra head's-up.

There's a myriad of theories as to why our young adults aren't learning to cook, even though there is a new fascination with the cooking world (thank you Food Network and now others)!

One of the biggest and most overlooked reasons our teens aren't cooking, is that parents don't want to burden them with a job the parent feels he or she is responsible for!

Parents… it's true, your kids are swamped with activities, sports, and schoolwork! But, the reality is parents are swamped too! If this generation of parents doesn't involve our young adults with cooking at home, we may actually be loving them to death!

What are the Watermarks? Use 'em or Don't!

Only YOU know whether or not the watermarks are useful in your home!

The watermarks are essentially helping your kitchen run like a smooth and well managed chef's kitchen.

A great chef leaves clear directions for his prep crew. His or her restaurant flourishes because he is creative but his best asset is his ability to delegate! His restaurant will thrive and his rewards will be pride and profit! Your home will thrive and your profit will be peace, understanding, compassion, health and yes, even cash because you are going to save a ton of it!

If you already do a great deal of cooking at home and have taught your young adults how to cook... You will love the idea of Cooking Together/ Apart™! The watermarks will enhance your cooking experience. A quick glance at the "Prep Crew" sticky note the night before, reminds you what meat to take out and what to delegate.

prep crew

- brown meat
- cut toppings
- assemble

stove-top

If you are a young adult and love to cook...
You can become the head chef or delegator. No matter your career or job choice, you will rise to the top with this skill set! The ability to delegate effectively will make you stand out in the workforce.

If you, like most, have always been the main cook and others don't know how to help out...
The watermarks and sticky note combo will become your best friends! I suggest in this case you start by taking 5 minutes the night before to cut or chop and set the stuff aside in the fridge. Get someone else to assemble. If you are comfortable with your young adults using the stove even better. They can have it ready when you get home.

You are roommates (college students or working) or a young couple... You eat out way too much and it's costing your body and your pocketbook a fortune! You want to learn to stay healthy and save money. Cooking Together/Apart™ can help you achieve this and the sticky note will be invaluable for knowing who's doing what!

> *Your home will thrive and your profit will be peace, understanding, compassion, health and yes, even cash because you are going to save a ton of it!*

The next page is for teens only... no peeking! ⟶

Teens… lend me your ears for a minute! You need to cook and you need to cook at least one or two meals a week! Why? So you can take care of yourself when you move out in a few years! Think… independence! And, did you know, you're more likely to have a better body image and actually be healthier the more you cook for yourself? It's true! But, shhhh, there's a little problem standing in the way! Your parents!

Sooooo, while you are easing your parents into this transition of your independence and healthy future, just let them cut stuff up the night before if it makes them feel more comfortable, ok? That way, you can just throw it all together when you get home from school. And, if they ask you to wait until they get home to turn on the stove or oven, just smile and nod…remember they're old and you're young! Patience! LOL

I know they didn't let you buy that crazy shirt. You weren't allowed to go to the party without parental supervision and they won't let you pierce the 5th earring into your navel or get a tattoo… but, they love you, they really do! They're afraid you're going to cut or burn yourself. That's right! Like it or not, they really like you! That's why you have to take control and let them know they can stop feeling guilty about you getting dinner started once or twice a week before they get home (if you get there first).

Truth or Consequence?

University students, teens and preteens: You can change your eating world for the better within your family environment. In the meantime, you will feel fantastic and inspired. In fact, you will feel better than you've ever felt! Are you ready for some truths?

Truth 1– We screwed up your food! Sorry! Ever since the industrial revolution parents have searched for ways to have more time with their kids. They have allowed the food industry to pull on their emotional heartstrings, trading their family's health for time!

Truth 2– Chances are most of you are the first generation to be eating processed food 24/7! Your organs are freaking out and as a result it's affecting your moods. Feeling sad, tired and overwhelmed shouldn't be the norm. It should be the exception!

Truth 3– Studies show that the more you cook at home the better you will feel! You will feel more independent, likely get better grades, have a better body image and feel more secure when moving out on your own when that time comes.

Truth 4– Your parents love you! They are overwhelmed living in a complex world trying to be the best parent they can be, yet always feeling like they are falling short... especially when it comes to getting dinner on the table! They are confused and most don't even know what healthy means anymore! All they know is that they are out of time when dinnertime comes around! So, they often opt for fast-food or convenient processed packaged food.

Truth 5– Parents will likely not ask you to cook. They feel guilty about having you do something they think they are responsible for. Their decision to choose quick processed food is a spontaneous decision based on their feelings of being overwhelmed!

Truth 6– Parents are scared you might burn down the house or cut yourself if you don't usually cook. This adds to their feelings of being overwhelmed!

The Importance of Family Dinner

We sit down to the table and one of our daughters is clearly having a bad day. She says she's not hungry. Her exaggerated shoulder slouch is grouchy body language personified! It's screaming, "Why do I have to sit here with my doorknob parents and siblings…grrrrrr!" The rest of the family continues to fill up their plates and she reluctantly decides to serve a tiny bit for herself. The conversation begins and with each and every subject she snaps back an unarguable comment. Finally, a sister sibling blurts out loudly, "Knock it off, it's not my fault Jeremy broke up with you!" The room goes silent. She screams to the top of her lungs, "I can't believe you just said that!" She pushes her chair out, stomps upstairs and slams her door!!! It's uncomfortable for a bit but then the conversation begins again. We clean up. I set aside a plate for her, put the teakettle on and bring a cup to her room. I knock on the door and she screams, "I don't want you to come in!" I let her know that I have simply brought her a tea and that I'll be ready to talk when she is. She accepts. I no sooner get past the chair and before I know it the tears burst through her overstressed tear ducts! She runs behind me and slams the door shut so no one will hear her cry. I'm not sure if at that point she realized she trapped me in with her. I do know, that an hour flashed by in a moment, and I learned all about her pain. A hug and a sob. I pray I've said the right thing and then I hear a distant clunk of the fridge door. My girl is hungry.

Now, you're probably thinking... *Is Sandi trying to convince us to have dinner together or to avoid it?* Here's the thing; I found out something that night I might not have known for days, had we not been having dinner together! When you eat dinner together, the pulse of the family is present! On good days and on bad days, like this one! I'm not a perfect parent and didn't always handle situations well (and sometimes I downright handled them wrong). But, in our crazy world of chaos and confusion there was one constant, one thing everyone could count on… dinner together!

That's just one of many stories that kept reminding me over the years how important dinner together is. That's why it's sooo important that families are Cooking Together/Apart™ in the workweek, so that being healthy, both physically and mentally has a fighting chance! If you're looking for evidence from research for eating dinner together, the truth lies below.

Eating together at home often results in...

Better concentration at work or school

Better grades

Better body image

... and you are

Less likely to abuse drugs

Less likely to abuse alcohol

More likely to have better social skills

More likely to have a higher self esteem

Are You Feeling Sad, Sluggish or Misunderstood?

Do you ever wake up in the morning and think: life sucks? Well surprise, surprise, you're not alone! We live in a fast paced world filled with conflicting opinions, options and information about life and about what we put into our bodies! There are all kinds of things that can make a person feel sluggish including stress! But sometimes I wonder which came first, the chicken or the egg? Stress has always been there and will always be there. Without stress we would never be able to experience what feeling "amazing" is like! But, how can it be that in such a short period of time, in only a few generations, we have gone from feeling pretty great about life, to feeling pretty confused and anxious! Record numbers of teens and young adults are complaining of sleep disorders, deep depression, anxiety and an inability to focus or live in the now! Browse the internet and take a look at the countless studies that show us that although food may not be the only source of our sluggishness all the time, it's definitely a key factor. Whether you are slim or overweight… what you eat can make you feel sad, sluggish, misunderstood or depressed! Really... really!

The media and health industry seem to be obsessed with pointing the finger at a person who looks unhealthy not the person who **is** unhealthy! This is creating a ton of confusion as to what healthy and unhealthy even means anymore! Do you know that we don't even allow the word "obesity" into our school program, cKinect-Ed? This is because for every overweight person, there is a skinny person eating all the wrong things. They think they will never become overweight and that they are healthy!!! But in actuality, many are fat on the inside, and eventually that's coming out somewhere!

> Whether you are slim or overweight… what you eat can make you feel sad, sluggish, misunderstood or depressed! Really... really!

I personally believe, based on my 18 years experience, that the most important thing we should be looking at is not so much the fat, sugar and salt we cook with at home (in reasonable doses), but rather the fat, sugar and salt in the processed ready-to-eat foods we don't ever think about.

I'm not a doctor who studies nutrition, but here's what I know for sure. Over the years I have watched people's lives literally transform, get happier, in short order by making a few simple adjustments in how they eat, drink and move!

Now here's the cool part - I can actually help you to simplify your eating life. As a result, you and the people around you are going to feel a whole lot better! This is going to mean you won't feel like life sucks nearly as much and possibly hardly at all.

So let's delve into some of the topics we hear about and try to make sense of some of them. We'll use the, "**What they say**" and, "**What they mean**" meter!

Are You Feeling Sad, Sluggish or Misunderstood?

Your Liver is Like a Washing Machine!

I believe the young adults of today can literally change our society's eating habits for the better, in ten short years! Buuut, we have to trust them, and then let them! When I speak to students at their schools around the country, I begin with two simple questions. "Why do you think I'm here?" The answer fills the room with a drawl of synchronized boredom: "Tooo maaaake uuus eeeeeat heaaaalthy!" I respond, "No, I'm not here to make you eat healthy. In fact, I'm here as a representative of my generation, and a couple of generations past, to apologize for messing up your food!" Their backs straighten. Then I ask, "If I told you how to eat healthy would you trust me?" A resounding "NO" cries out with slightly more vigor!

We're not getting to these young brilliant adults because they don't trust us! They don't trust us because we have been immersed in fast food and convenience and we aren't doing what we tell them to do! They see the boxed foods in the freezer. They go along for the pizza pick up! They don't get the healthy message because they can't relate to it. It's not what they see in their real world. Teens and young adults are smart. They know it's lip service, not truth and all they want is truth! Sooo, the following pages are for them! (Ok, I guess you can read it too!) Here's the truth about what the heck is going on inside a human body, when you eat certain foods, in a way I hope you understand. What you do with that information afterwards is up to you!

> Your liver is the master organ in charge of getting nutrition to 50 trillion cells in your body. It's not meant to handle high quantities of processed foods.

What they say: Fast food and processed foods are bad for you!
What they mean: In short, your liver is the master organ in charge of getting nutrition to 50 trillion cells in your body. It's not meant to handle high quantities of processed foods. It also transforms toxins into bile so that you can poop out the bad stuff! It does more, but let's just say your liver is kind of like a washing machine (but better).

Soooo... imagine throwing tar and gunk all over your clothes then stuffing them into a washing machine. Now imagine running that washing machine, over and over, so that it never ever stops. But in between every few loads, you throw more tar and gunk in and turn it on again! Sounds crazy, right? The machine would stop functioning properly and eventually break down, "get tired"! Well, when we keep stuffing our bodies with junk, the liver keeps working to get rid of it and over time it can't do the job it's intended to do efficiently. The rest of your body, including your thyroid, suffers and you feel lousy!

Are You Feeling Sad, Sluggish or Misunderstood?

What they say: - Don't eat high fat food!

What they mean: - If you eat a lot of take-out or boxed processed foods, your arteries will not be working as well as they should.

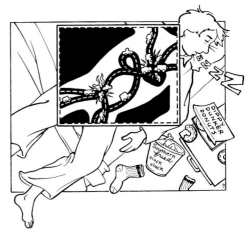

Imagine you have two tubes: one you pour water into, then you let it dry. The other, you pour corn syrup into, then you let it dry. The water represents the good fat HDL and the corn syrup represents the bad fat LDL. You pour more water into the water tube once it's dry and pour more corn syrup into the corn syrup tube once it's dry. With a microscope, you will be able to see faint deposits left on the tube by the water, but the tube will be wide open for business. However, the naked eye will clearly show the corn syrup tube starting to close!

The truth is, blood vessels (arteries) carry blood and oxygen to the heart and you don't want to mess with that. These microscopic, soft, waxy specks floating around in your bloodstream are called HDL and LDL. The good cholesterol is HDL (think H for Happy) and the bad is LDL (think L for Lardy).

How do you know what good fats and bad fats are?

From a research point of view, the more liquid the fat, the better it is! But, it doesn't mean you don't eat some of the other stuff… it's a matter of how much of it you're eating! Think "M for moving" fat (monounsaturated good fat). It's in stuff like canola oil, olive oil and peanut oil. Think "P for pacing" fat (polyunsaturated fats or fairly good fats). Corn, safflower and sunflower oils are good examples of these. Think "S for stationary" fat (saturated fats). Saturated fats are considered a bad fat, however, in moderation, many of the foods associated with it can bring other great nutrients to your body! Foods like meat, cheese and some tropical oils are examples. Remember, there's a lot of food in this category that's good for you. It's your job to make sure your diet isn't full of fat and when eating fat you eat more good than bad. Think "T for trouble, terrible and tired" fat (trans fat - really bad fat). This fat appears in tons of stuff we eat in take-out, boxed foods, cookies, crackers and much more. Not only is this fat saturated, it's also processed… noooot a good thing for your body! Buyer beware! Just because a label says no trans fats, doesn't mean you're eating healthy fat.

Real food, in the right quantities, will get you all the nutrients you need. If my plate were split in three, I would have half the plate with salads, fruits or veggies, a quarter filled with rice, quinoa, bread or pasta and a quarter (or fist size) of meat or protein.

If you eat bad fat consistently, over time, the blood and oxygen can't get to the heart efficiently. When that happens, you feel sluggish, tired and lousy! This often leads you to lie on the couch or sit in your room and that helps the bad fat stick even more! Ouch, the truth hurts!

Are You Feeling Sad, Sluggish or Misunderstood?

Sugar, the new buzzword! But what does it mean?

What they say: Sugar is bad for you! Don't eat sugar! Each one of us is eating on average 130-155 lbs of sugar every year.

What they mean: Stop eating processed foods and ridiculous amounts of sweetened drinks!

The "Super Biggie!" is giving you over 3/4 of a cup of sugar and even the "Super!" is over 1/3 cup!

Companies that process food hide sugar in almost everything so that you will buy their food! (Because sugar is like a drug; the more you eat the more you want!) Drink companies make their drinks sweeter and sweeter so they seem tastier to you. Stores then offer deals for large quantities of the sweet drinks. They don't do this because they like you and want to make you happy... buuut, because they want you to go to their store and buy other things!!!

Here's the deal on processed food, sugar and drinks: If you didn't make it yourself, with real food, you are probably eating waaaay too much sugar. If you are eating take-out or boxed processed food, a lot of you are likely eating copious amounts of sugar. If you are having a sweet drink with that, you are likely feeling tired, sad and slowly teaching your body to crave more sugar! (Which will make you more sick and tired and eventually will likely kill you! Harsh, I know, but you need the truth!)

When you eat take out or processed pizza, hamburgers, hotdogs, fried chicken, fish, meat pies, preseasoned meat at the grocer, salads, soups or even some meats that are previously frozen; do you think you are eating sugar? Probably not, but you are! (And I haven't even touched on desserts, sweetened drinks or take-out yet!) The message from the media is sooo confusing! You are hearing that the actual sugar we're using at home is the problem. The reality is that people who cook at home most of the time, using mostly real food, often have no problem with sugar, and yes they use it!

If you, the brilliant young adults of our nation, put your foot down and insist that you help out with cooking at home, for your own sake, I believe it's the first crucial step toward escaping your generation's sugar addiction!

Are You Feeling Sad, Sluggish or Misunderstood?

Do you really WANT to feel great? I mean do you really?

Getting back to the drinks for a minute! In 2003 I had the honor of working with Dr. Kelly Brett and Dr. George Lambrose. Both are respected sport's physicians and surgeons based out of Calgary, Alberta, Canada. They have a passion for teaching people about proper nutrition. When we worked together on my book, *The Healthy Family*, some people were shocked by the picture I asked our illustrator to draw of a young adult peeing out her bones. I wanted the picture to say what the docs were saying in words: "The phosphates in the soda drinks actually bind to calcium and it gets peed out of our bodies!" Wow! Isn't that yet another great reason to drink soda pop?

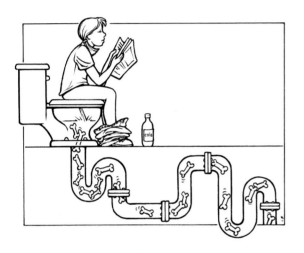

In contrast, I love what the docs said about getting hooked on water. Water boosts your energy, helps you think better, plays a role in transmitting messages within the brain to the muscles and lubricates your body parts. Seriously!!! Hey, you are the smart generation of young adults…you tell me what you should be drinking!

A few years back, this amazing woman, named Elise, decided to help a group of teen girls in our community. She wanted them to feel better and accept the way their bodies looked. She asked me to come and talk to the girls about helping out with dinner in their homes. The girls were also challenged to grab a bottle of water every time they felt like soda pop. Within weeks the girls reported having more energy, most lost weight and all of them said they would never go back to regularly drinking soda pop or sweet drinks again because of how great they felt!!!

"Challenges are what make life interesting; overcoming them is what makes life meaningful!"
- Joshua J. Marine

"Accept challenges, so that you may feel the exhilaration of Victory!"
- George S. Patton

I thought I would throw these out before you decide to ditch out before the little challenge I have for you!

If you Really want to feel great, I mean if you really want to…

- Cook at least one meal recipe each week for the next three weeks.
- Eat one bite of something you're not crazy about, when you or someone else cooks.
- Grab a bottle or glass of water every time you crave a soda pop.
- Share how great you feel with your friends, then support each other to feel great!

What to Make For Dinner?

Did you know that not having the right ingredients to make a meal is the #2 reason families regularly don't eat a healthy dinner at home? A "grab anything" dinner always starts with not knowing what to have for dinner!

Did you know the number #1 reason the ingredients aren't in the house is that your parent, or the usual cook, doesn't know what to make for dinner? Here's why! Everyone has different likes and dislikes and the usual cook's schedule is likely over the top busy! (between work and parenting obligations like sports, laundry, lunches, house cleaning…belieeeeve me, the list is loooong!) So within that chaos, the decision to choose the meal is often something that keeps being forgotten until… dinner! Dinner also happens to be the time when everyone is hungry and tired! It's actually the most stressful time of the day for most families because although one part of the day ends, another part of the day begins! Doesn't sound like a great time to be figuring out what to make for dinner, does it?

> ## A "grab anything" dinner always starts with not knowing what to have for dinner!

Do you hear what I'm saying? If you help pick a meal or two and then write your choice down on the top left corner of our grocery list at sandirichard.com, you have no idea how much that one small action will help a parent, roommate, partner or whoever is the usual cook or shopper. It will clear that person's head and the, "What to Make" for dinner dilemma will be gone. **Knowing what to make for dinner removes a ton of stress. And not just at dinner, but all day long!**

There's another reason for doing the next steps. Everyone becomes aware of what dinner is at the start of the day. When you know what you're eating for dinner, you don't feel like eating similar things during the day. This automatically balances out what you're eating. Balance makes your body feel better and stay healthier. I call this Eating Forward™.

Five Easy Steps to Help Make Dinner the Best Part of Your Day!

#1. Go to **sandirichard.com**. Click on Grocery List Generator in the menu bar and then **click on the Blank Eat Sheet tab**.

#2. Write down what you feel like having for one or two dinners and get other people in your family to write their choices too! Make sure you write which page of the recipe book it's on right beside your choice. Make sure the meals are not all the same or too similar. You need a variety of meals to keep your week nutritionally balanced! If two people have chosen something similar, just pick something else you like.

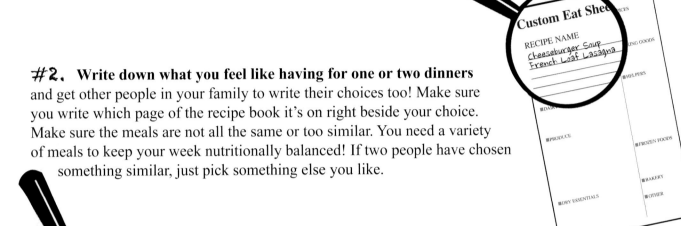

#3. Once all five are chosen, the parent or usual shopper can easily sit down and **transfer each ingredient from the meal recipe to the blank Eat Sheet™**. Remind them …DO NOT LEAVE INGREDIENTS OFF THE LIST EVEN IF YOU HAVE THEM IN THE HOUSE. You want a complete list, a reusable Eat Sheet™. That way, for these five meals your family will never have to do this work again.

#4. Anyone can now use this Eat Sheet™ to walk around and **check the fridge, freezer and cupboards to know which groceries you will need to purchase** at the grocery store, to make those five meals. The cool thing about the Eat Sheet™ is that it is so complete! Anyone can use it to make a shopping list for those meals any week of the year!

23

Here's a suggestion to make life even easier…

Keep the complete eat sheet in a plastic sheet protector and put that in a small binder close to the recipe books. Make sure EVERYONE knows where it is. That way anyone can grab it to make a grocery list at any time.

Each week you follow these steps you will add a new Eat Sheet™ to your binder.
Oooor, if you are mostly using our books, I'd get the ESG grocery list generator so that the grocery lists are all made for you!

Once you really get into this and you're on a roll, go get some different colored sticky tabs. As soon as someone masters a meal recipe, pick a color and "tab it": John's green, Chris is yellow. When things are crazy rushed and you don't have time to do an Eat Sheet, your tabs will make it really easy for the usual shopper to know which meals you know how to make. They easily can go pick up the groceries. You can sort out who's doing what and when, later!

Tab it!

Shannon   Nick   Chris   Dad

5.   Go buy your groceries!

Cooking Lingo

Add to uncleaned bowl - You don't need to rinse the bowl you just used.

Bake - placing something in a preheated oven

Beat - to mix together fast using an electric mixer or whisk; recipe will often give instructions or instruct

Boil - the liquid will bubble up

Broil - Turn top oven element on to brown or crisp the top of food. Never take your eyes off the broiling food. It can very quickly burn what you have made.

Brown ground meat - Break it up with a spoon in a stove-top pan until it's not pink and looks crumbled.

Brush - to cover something using a cooking brush made of natural fibers or heat proof plastic

Coat - to completely cover something like chicken in flour or crumbs

Combine or Mix - to make all the ingredients come together

Cut meat into thin strips against the grain - Cut across the lines you see in the meat.

Cut or chop - instructions in recipes will explain how to cut (into large chunks or small chunks)

Cover - to evenly distribute something on top like grated cheese or mashed potatoes

Drain - to remove the water from something steamed or boiled, usually using a colander in the sink

Drizzle - to add an ingredient sparingly such as oil, or dressings

Fill a large pot with water - enough for the pasta you are cooking, usually about half way or more

Finely Cut or Dice - very small pieces

Flip - to turn the meat or veggie to the other side to brown

Heat oil - Oil should be hot before adding food. If you're new at this, get ahead with the cutting.

Julienne - to cut very thin pieces lengthwise. Buy a julienne peeler. It's just like a potato peeler…easy!!

Layer - to put one ingredient on top of another

Melt - to turn solid into liquid, as in melting butter

Rinse - to remove surface dirt from veggies or lettuce

Sautè - to cook something in oil, in a stove-top pan

Simmer - to very slowly cook at a lower temperature

Slice - is another way of saying cut and indicates how thick, thin or how long to slice

Sliver - to slice thinly, but not as thin as julienne

Smear (or spread) - to evenly cover something usually with a sauce or paste

Soften - to make something softer without melting it, like peanut butter or cream cheese

Sprinkle - to distribute something like cheese or spice evenly over something

Stir In - to stir into the existing mixture

Toss until meat is no longer pink - turning cut up chicken, beef or pork with a spoon while it turns brown

Trim - to take the parts off you don't want on meat or veggie

Unroll or unravel chicken thigh - To flatten out. You can still scrunch it together in a pan to fit.

Whisk - to create a smooth texture using a whisk. If using a fork, you need to stir very quickly.

Do I Really Have To Buy THAT Ingredient?

"I am not buying a whole jar of THAT ingredient for one recipe; what am I ever going to use it for again!" Would you buy a bag of flour if you were baking a cake? What about the cocoa, baking soda, baking powder and whatever else is needed for the cake? Whatever the reason when we skip out on buying the proper ingredients for a meal and it doesn't turn out... we say the recipe didn't work!

I am very sensitive when it comes to getting people to buy ingredients. You can almost always find the ones my recipes use in a grocery store and they have many uses. Sauces, condiments, oils and spices last a really long time. Once you own them, you will fall in love with their many uses. Chances are if you are attracted to a certain recipe in the first place, other recipes, like it, will ask for similar ingredients in different amounts such as Asian, Mexican, Indian or Italian cuisine. Not only will buying the ingredient add to the success of your meal recipe, but also you'll love it when it's around for a different one. Here's my list of… **What to buy and how to use them!**

Spices you don't normally use - like curry powder or garam masala. I have turned thousands of people onto grocery store variety North American curry powder. Remember, curry isn't a spice it's a combination of spices so check the ingredients. It probably contains spices you already use and love. The right spice can really make a difference in a recipe. A dark cupboard makes them last a reeeally long time!

Sesame seeds - make almost anything look great! Toasted sesame seeds have more absorbable calcium so either buy them toasted or make sure they are being toasted, which they are if you are baking them on top of something.

Panko flakes - are dry, fine, white Japanese bread crumbs. They are mostly used for crunchy coatings! They are easy to find at your grocer in the coating mix aisle.

Corn flake crumbs - can be purchased all crushed up. You find them in the coating mix aisle. We always bake our coatings on meat or veggies, rather than deep fry. I personally find the cornflake crumbs come out a little crunchier and tastier than panko flakes in most cases. If you only want to buy one or the other, I'd get the cornflake crumbs.

Salsa - can be added to almost any sauce for flavor and texture. It stores great in the fridge with a fairly long expiry. It doesn't last long if it's market chopped or homemade.

Pesto - is amazing as a pizza base instead of tomato sauce. I use a dab or two to grill my veggies instead of using oil and it's a fabulous flavor booster for any creamed pasta sauce. It has a fairly long expiry date but once you see how versatile it is, it won't last!

Dijon mustard - is a great addition to Mediterranean, French or Italian style sauces. It adds an interesting depth of flavor. It's there, but it's not! It's also great on sandwiches!

Soy sauce - can add a salty flavor and dark color to many dishes. But like salt—not too much! It stores beautifully in the pantry with a long expiry date!

Sweet Thai chili sauce - I have so many people tell me this one sauce has become a staple in their fridge! It's great when you want to add a little sweetness and heat to a dish. It's a mild heat with a lovely sweet flavor. I use this in Asian and Indian dishes. I combine it with hot sauce to balance the heat, yet kick up the flavor on grilled chicken and wings.

Kepac Manis - (sweet soy sauce found in the authentic Asian section of grocer) an amazing condiment to add to any stir fry or Asian dish. It's thick, sweet and salty. Mostly used in Asian cuisine, it has a long expiry date.

Sambal Oelek - (hot chili sauce or garlic-chili sauce) a tiny bit is all you need to spice up any sauce. It's stored in the fridge and has a very long expiry.

Maple syrup - one of the most amazing natural sweeteners for sauces or dressings. It store's in the fridge long term. It is expensive, but a little goes a long way and lasts a looong time… sooooo it's not that expensive in the long run!

Peanut butter - is a great substitute for recipes that require you to purée nuts for a recipe. It's a quick way to speed up preperation and add complex flavor to Asian and Indian dishes.

Chocolate milk syrup - can really be a quick addition to molé (the sauce, not the animal) or any dish that adds the complex flavor of chocolate. It stores beautifully for a long time and is a great way to get milk into your kids.

Hot pepper relish - fantastic added to anything you want to give texture and heat to. Add to mayonnaise for a hot tartar sauce. Fabulous on hot dogs! It stores long term in the fridge.

Olives - great as a pizza topping and wonderful to put out with a little oil and balsamic vinegar with bread for a quick appetizer when friends drop in.

Chicken, Beef, or Veggie broth - canned, long term storage; tetra pacs, larger size is more economical, but has a limited fridge life. Fantastic to add to almost anything. Purchase reduced-sodium when possible! I keep an oil marker in my knife drawer and mark the date when I open it up!

Vinegars - great for dressings, sauces and for dipping with oil of course. If your vinegar is cloudy, don't throw it out! It's called, "Mother of Vinegar"! This is the stuff chefs love!

Oils - Olive oil is great for savory dishes as well as dressings, sautéing veggies, combining with balsamic vinegar for dipping bread, drizzling on cooked pasta so it doesn't stick and more. It's also one of the good fats! It stores reasonably well at room temp, but like any oil, if you don't use a lot, buy smaller quantities so it's always fresh. Canola, vegetable and peanut oil are great for any dish where you don't want added flavor. Sesame oil is great for sautéing as well as flavoring many Asian dishes!

Garlic or ginger - (from a jar or tube) are great to have on hand during the work week for those days when you get in a traffic jam and have to help Johnny with his 12 hour school project but only have 4 hours! I use this during the workweek all the time!

Cheese - Cambozola is a very mild creamy blue cheese. Amazing on chicken burgers and hamburgers or scattered on pizza with caramelized onion. Gruyere is expensive but an amazing treat! It's my all time favorite cheese with a sharp but sweet flavor! Ricotta can be added to almost any cream sauce or filling!

No Burns, No Cuts...
Great chefs know how to keep their kitchens safe.

Oven Mitts
Long comfortable oven mitts are a must for any well prepared chef. I would never take the chance of getting burnt!

Apron or T-shirt
If you think wearing an apron is not for you, then find a favorite old T-Shirt. Short sleeves are the key so that fabric isn't dangling over a hot stove. The point of an apron is to protect your good clothes.

Clutter
Only the pans you're cooking with should ever be on the stove-top. Clutter can confuse even a great cook and it can be dangerous!

Microwave-safe Pot for Rice
Make sure you put a paper towel underneath. When you remove it from the microwave, use oven mitts—it's HOT! If you have an electric rice cooker that can cook your rice in 20 minutes, or be adjusted to your meal, go ahead and use that.

Electric Fry Pan
If you are a new cook, and living at home, parents may feel more comfortable if you are using an electric fry pan at first!

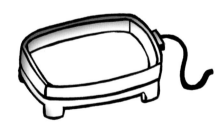

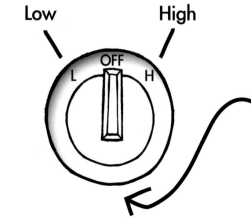

Low   **High**

OFF

L   H

High, Medium & Low on Your Oven
If your oven dial only has markings for **High** (H) or **Low** (L) and we say **Medium**, it's in the middle of the two. **Medium-Low** is closer to the low. If something is taking you longer to cut the first time you do a meal recipe, use common sense and pull your pan off the heat occasionally so you don't overcook.

No Burns, No Cuts...

Pots and Pans
Always use oven mitts when removing lids or removing pots from the heat. If you think something is overcooking, don't get nervous. Just slide it off the heat if you are using an electric stove. Turn off the heat for a gas or electric fry pan.

Fry Pan Handles
Make sure you turn the pan handles inward. It can be both dangerous and disappointing if your creation accidentally gets knocked off and goes flying.

Cutting and Slicing
Always tuck your fingers back when cutting. Use your knuckles as a guide. It feels weird at first, but practice makes it feel normal pretty quickly. Notice that the thumb is tucked slightly behind the curled back tips of your fingers.

Dials & Knobs
If knobs on your stove don't clearly indicate which burner it's for, label them with a label maker or even tape.

TOP LEFT

Turn Burner & Oven Off
Don't forget to turn the burners and oven off. It should always be your last safety check. Oil and food left behind on a burner or in the oven can start a fire. Also, if you are cooking for people who aren't home yet, turn everything off, slide your meal off the hot burners or take baked meals out of the oven, then cover with foil. You can always heat things up when everyone is home! If they take way longer to get home than expected, place in fridge once it's cooled down a bit.

Building a House Requires Tools...
So Does Making Dinner!

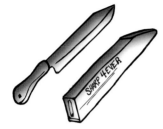

Sharp Knives

If you can afford to buy a few great knives, great! A great way to keep them sharp is by using a pull through diamond wheel. If you can't afford to buy a good knife, buy the kind that self-sharpens when you return it into its holder. A sharp knife will make dinner making easier.

2 cutting boards & 2 knives

When cooking dinner, use a separate cutting board for your veggies and meat. Put a dampened cloth underneath to stop the board from slipping as you cut. It's a good idea to have two sharp knives, one for vegetables and one for meat.

Julienne Peeler

My sister Janice introduced me to the julienne peeler. It works just like a potato peeler, but juliennes. I use it all the time now. Thanks Jan!

Vegetable Chopper

Vegetable choppers are great for new cooks and experienced cooks. Use it especially if something needs fine chopping.

Cheese Grater

It's ok to purchase preshredded cheese from time to time. You will notice a difference though when shredding your own in your own combinations. I like the grater with four sides. I find it easier to hold, and it has a variety of grates on each side.

2 sets of Measuring Cups & Spoons

Two sets of measuring cups and spoons out will make your dinner making way easier (one for dry and one for wet). You won't need both everytime you cook, but when you do, it speeds up the task.

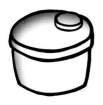

Salad Spinner

I use my salad spinner for rinsing all sorts of fruits and veggies including lettuce leaves then spinning them dry. I can't live without it!

Whisk

A whisk is a kitchen necessity when making sauces on a stove-top. You can use a fork too, but you will really notice the difference a whisk makes. They only cost a few bucks!

Pots, Pans & Baking Pans

Using the right size pot, fry pan or baking pan in a recipe can make all the difference. Using a lid makes water boil faster. If you don't have a lid, you can pick up a universal one at a large grocery store.

Timer

Use a seperate timer and time yourself making dinner. Don't start until all your stuff's out and then it's fun to track how efficient you're getting.

Thermometers

I don't understand why everyone doesn't own two different types of meat thermometers. An oven-safe thermometer is one that you leave in your meat while it's cooking.

An instant read thermometer checks smaller things like the internal temperature of a hamburger, chicken breast or piece of fish. Home cooks often get nervous about not cooking their meat enough so they overcook it and dry it out! For a few dollars and the click of a button, you never have to guess. And, your meat will always be moist! Tab this page for your internal meat temps.

| Beef and Lamb Medium rare 140°F Well done 160°F | Chicken breasts or thighs 165-170°F | Pork chops or Roast Medium 140°F Well-done 160°F | Ground meats 160-165°F | Fish filets 140°F Tuna 125°F |

Important:

When using an electric stove-top, remember many recipes are tested in test kitchens using a gas stove-top. If the recipe says reduce to medium, you likely have to slide your pan off the heat first, reduce the heat and then put it back on in a few minutes. All ovens do not heat equally. It's always a good idea to check your oven from time to time with an easy to purchase oven thermometer. Sometimes it may need a repairman for a slight adjustment.

Little Tricks for Best Results

Cutting Flank for Stir-Fry

I'm known for being a huge fan of flank or skirt steaks for use in stir-frys, fajitas and so on. I always say sirloin or flank because you can't always get flank. But here's why I love it so much. It's so easy for the home cook to see the fibers of the meat. When you see the fibers, it's easier to cut across them, which shortens the fiber, making each piece more tender.

First, cut long strips parallel to the lines.

Then slice thin strips crossing the fiber.

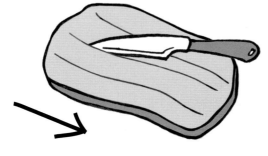

Spreading Mashed Potatoes

Use a fork to spread mashed potatoes on top of something like Shepherd's Pie, so it's much easier. If you want to finish up the look with the back of a spoon for smoothness, go ahead.

Cooking Noodles Separately for Soups

You will notice we never cook our noodles or rice in soups anymore. I have learned over the years that it's so much better to cook them separately. When you put your noodles or rice into the bottom of your bowl, pour your hot soup over top. The noodles or rice always taste fresh and never mushy! I also find it to be quite economical. I will often make soup when I know I have leftover pasta or rice and just use what I have!

> ### I love how Cooking Together/Apart™ helps families work together (even when they're apart)!
>
> I strongly recommend cutting or chopping the meat, onion or anything else you can get to, the night before. That will help whoever is cooking the next day. Try not to spend more than 10 minutes so that you don't end up overwhelmed in the midst of busyness. Those few minutes will go a long way to getting a great dinner on the table and creating a feeling that someone else helped out!

Prepping & Cutting For Speed

Forming a meatloaf for quick cooking

How to butterfly chicken the easy way

chicken breast

squish chicken breast

slice in half, but not all the way through

open up

Prepping & Cutting For Speed

How to pick and cut a pepper

Pick it up in the palm of your hand. The lighter it is, the more hollow it is.
Why would you want to pay for all the stuff inside it when you just throw it out anyways?

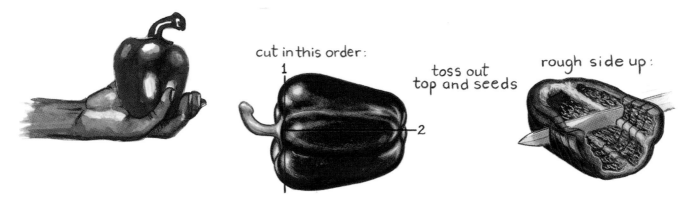

cut in this order:
1
2

toss out
top and seeds

rough side up:

How to cut green onion

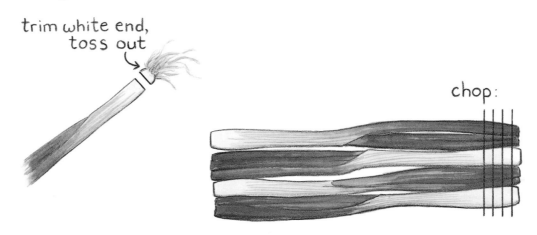

trim white end,
toss out

chop:

How to cut an onion

trim one end:

cut in half:

peel:

follow the grain to sliver:

cut again to dice:

34

Prepping & Cutting For Speed

How to cut a mushroom

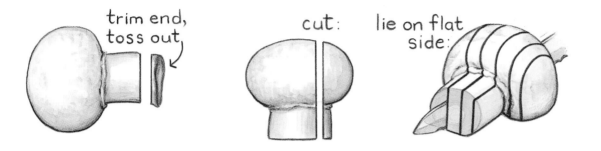

trim end, toss out

cut:

lie on flat side:

How to prepare asparagus

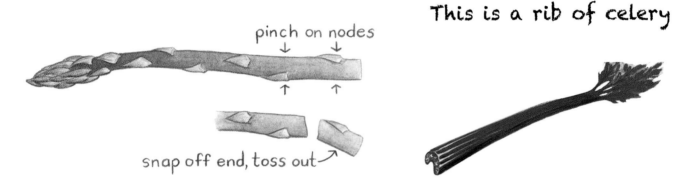

pinch on nodes

snap off end, toss out

This is a rib of celery

The difference between broccoli heads and florets

Food Guides

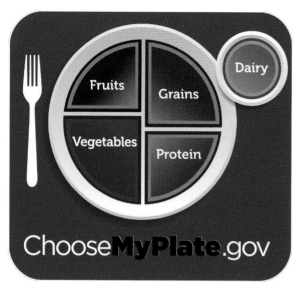

I believe, as I always have, that the Food Guides are right on track. The problem has been the people reading them!

Sooo…both the USDA ChooseMyPlate and Canada's Food Guide can now be personalized to your needs by going to their websites.

Before, the guides didn't know how much exercise you got. They didn't know anything about you, so it was your responsibility to follow the guides according to your specific information. Now they do the thinking for you.

You key in your information and they provide you with a plan customized to your needs. If you cut my plate into three parts, half would be veggies and fruits. The other half of the plate would be split between protein and grains. That's how the guide works for me. Why? Because I only manage to exercise three times a week, and the rest of the time I am standing at a kitchen counter or working at a computer. My daughter Paige, on the other hand, is far more active every day so she needs a few more grains than I do.

We also have to look at the guide from a financial standpoint. When the kids were little I purchased far more things like pasta and bread because it was inexpensive and I had to make my dollar stretch. But, I was running from morning 'til night and as a sanity break had a brisk walk every morning, so I was able to burn off what I ate. You can't go heavy on bread and sweets if you're sitting at a computer all day, come home, then sit on the couch. If you do that, you'll get fat and you can't blame the guides.

Go to **www.choosemyplate.gov** or **www.healthcanada.gc.ca/foodguide** and enjoy their new interactive approach to making your eating life easier to understand.

healthcanada.gc.ca/foodguide

36

Look Before You Cook

Here is why you look at a recipe ahead of time. How many times have you started to prepare a meal only to find out the meat needed to be marinated for at least an hour? Get the picture? That's why visual triggers such as the **Prep Code, Crescent Moon, Sticky Note and Take 5** are so helpful. These triggers will help you to match your meal to your schedule.

 **Prep Code** - see next page

At-A-Glance Sticky Note gives you the head's up for what meat to take out of the freezer and how to break up the tasks for the meal.

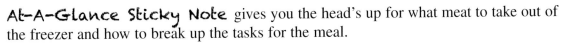 **A Crescent Moon** next to the clock reminds you to follow the 5 or 10 minute prep the night before so that the next day is ultra easy. Most of these can be started the same day, in the morning, if your schedule allows.

Take 5 - When you see this symbol take 5 minutes the night before to do a little cutting and chopping for the next night's meal. Remember, it's just a suggestion to make your life easier. Cooking Together/Apart personified!

I also include protein, carb and fruit-veggie symbols to the left of the instructions on each recipe. When you see a symbol - you'll know to shift to a different component of the whole dinner you are making.

●   Red circle = some type of protein

■   Blue square = some type of carbohydrate

▲   Green triangle = some type of fruit or vegetable

We named this icon **Carrot Top** (I know I'm a little looped in the brain). He helps people who want to eat less meat or are vegetarian. You can find him on the *About the Recipes* pages with directions telling you what to do to make the meal meatless. Take a look at page 40 and you will see what I mean.

Also...have fun with the rating page. Families love getting involved and it makes your life easier when you want to choose meals at a later date. You will see what I mean on page 41.

The Prep Code

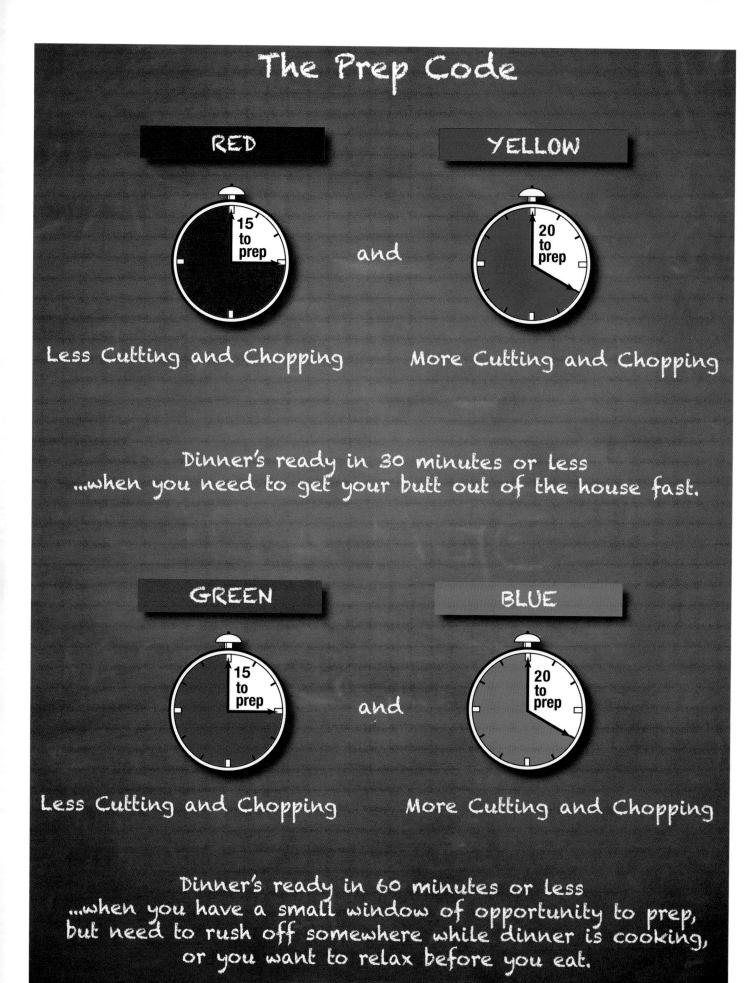

RED

15 to prep

Less Cutting and Chopping

and

YELLOW

20 to prep

More Cutting and Chopping

Dinner's ready in 30 minutes or less
...when you need to get your butt out of the house fast.

GREEN

15 to prep

Less Cutting and Chopping

and

BLUE

20 to prep

More Cutting and Chopping

Dinner's ready in 60 minutes or less
...when you have a small window of opportunity to prep,
but need to rush off somewhere while dinner is cooking,
or you want to relax before you eat.

The Chefs Rule Book:

Throw something on over your clothes, like an apron or a T-shirt

Take your stuff out, like Chefs do

Wash your hands before and after cutting meat

Use different cutting boards and different knives for meats and veggies

Always tuck your fingers back when cutting

Don't forget to turn off the stove-top or oven when you're done

Tab the meals you love with your own unique color tab, for easy reference

About The Recipes

Soft or Hard Shell Tacos

I don't think I have ever interviewed a family yet who didn't love tacos! These ones are easy to make and you don't need a package, just basic stuff from home.

Vegetarians, use veggie grind, but before you do, toss in a little mild curry powder (even if you don't like curry). You can't taste it, but it really makes a difference in the flavor of the tacos.

Chicken Caesar Pasta

I think this is my new favorite pasta! I just say the name and my mouth starts watering! It tastes sooo creamy, but it's low in fat and packed with flavor.

Vegetarians can cut up veggie based chicken strips.

Tomapplesauce Meatballs

I remember the first time I heard from a friend of mine that these ingredients were great together (tomato soup and applesauce), I thought it sounded disgusting. Take my word for it, it's well worth the try! I haven't met a kid who doesn't love these!

Note: Make sure you use extra-lean ground beef to keep the fat down.

Crunchy Orange Chicken

YUUUUUMMY!!! This is so mouth watering that, despite the fact that it's 5:00 a.m. as I write, my mouth is having a little fit! Note: There is a lot of liquid and you may feel something is wrong. There is nothing wrong. The beautiful liquid sucks itself up into the chicken and creates this amazing flavor. Our family tends to drizzle the remaining liquid on the potatoes!!! This dish is also great with rice.

Tuna Tetrazzini

Mac and cheese with a healthy twist. Simply cook the pasta the night before and toss in a little olive oil so it doesn't glob together. The kids can assemble the meal after school. Now that's cool!

If you are a vegetarian who doesn't eat fish, take it out and up the cheese a little.

Take 5 - Undercook your pasta the night before for a quick assembly-only meal.

Soft or Hard Shell Tacos with Toppings

Our Family Rating: 9.5

Your Family Rating: _____

Chicken Caesar Pasta with Peas

Our Family Rating: 10

Your Family Rating: _____

Tomapplesauce Meatballs with Rice and Broccoli

Our Family Rating: 8

Your Family Rating: _____

Crunchy Orange Chicken with Potatoes and Spinach Salad

Our Family Rating: 9.5

Your Family Rating: _____

Tuna Tetrazzini with Corn & Peas

Our Family Rating: 8

Your Family Rating: _____

TAKE

Red

Yellow

Yellow

Green

Green

Soft or Hard Shell Tacos with Toppings

Don't change yet! Take out equipment.

Take out ingredients.

1. Brown ground beef in large nonstick electric or stove-top **fry pan** at med-high until no longer pink.
   Add spice, ketchup and water to browned meat.

   Simmer meat mixture at medium-low.
   Meat mixture will thicken within 10 minutes.

<u>**Meat Mixture**</u>
1 lb or 450 g ground beef, extra lean

2 tsp chili powder
2 tsp onion flakes
1 tsp cumin powder
1/4 tsp turmeric
1/2 cup ketchup
1/2 cup water

2. Rinse lettuce in a salad spinner and spin dry. Chop green onion and cilantro and slice tomatoes.

   Set out toppings in small serving bowls on dinner table.

<u>**Toppings**</u>
1/4 head leaf lettuce
4 green onions
1/2 cup cilantro (optional)
4 Roma tomatoes

3. Spoon thickened meat mixture into tortilla and sprinkle with cheese.

   Add your favorite toppings.
   Roll up your tortilla, folding the bottom up to prevent leaking.

prepared meat mixture
6 soft flour, multigrain or corn tortillas, 10"
   (choose a lower sodium brand)
hard shell tacos (optional)
3/4 cup cheddar cheese, light, shredded
1/2 cup sour cream, fat-free or light
1/2 cup chunky salsa

This is such a fun and easy meal!

<u>**Serves 4-6**</u>

DINNER IS READY IN 30 MINUTES

Equipment List:

Large nonstick fry pan
Cutting board
Salad spinner
Cheese grater
4-6 small serving bowls
Sharp veggie knife
Mixing spoon
Measuring cups and spoons

Per serving:

Calories	378
Fat	10.2 g
Protein	26.1 g
Carbohydrate	46.9 g
Fiber	2.9 g
Sodium	774 mg

U.S. Food Exchanges:	Cdn. Food Choices:
2 1/2 Starch	3 Carb
3 Meat-lean	3 Meat/Alt
1/2 Other	

Prep Crew

- brown meat
- cut toppings
- assemble

Stove-top

15 to prep

Chicken Caesar Pasta with Peas

Don't change yet! Take out equipment.

Take out ingredients.

1. Fill a large **stove-top** pot with water and bring to a boil for pasta.
...meanwhile...

water

2. Heat oil in a large nonstick **fry** pan at medium. Cut chicken into small bite size pieces, adding to pan as you cut.
Add spice. Toss until meat is no longer pink. Add cream cheese, dressing and milk. Stir until cheese is melted and ingredients are combined. **Reduce heat** to low.
You may need to stir in a little more milk at the end, you want this thick but a little runny.

1 tsp olive oil, extra-virgin
3 chicken breasts, boneless, skinless
  (1 lb or 450 g)
1 tsp original, all purpose seasoning, salt-free
5 1/3 oz or 83 g cream cheese, light
  (just less that 3/4 of an 8 oz pack)
1/2 cup Caesar salad dressing, garlic lovers, light, gourmet, refrigerated
1 cup 1% milk

3. Place pasta in boiling water, stir and cook uncovered. Set timer according to package directions, approx 5 minutes.

12 oz or 340 g vermicelli pasta
  (use regular vermicelli or spaghettini, only use rice vermicelli if there are wheat allegeries in your family)

4. Place bacon on paper towel on plate in **microwave**. Set timer for 1 minute. Gently smash croutons with a mallet or kitchen hammer to create tiny croutons. Tear bacon into pieces. Set aside.

4 strips fully cooked bacon, low-sodium
  (purchase this way)
paper towel
1/2 cup croutons

5. Rinse peas in colander or steamer basket. Place water in the bottom of a **stove-top** pot and bring to a full boil with the peas in the basket above. Cover and set timer for 3 minutes...
...or microwave on high for 3-4 minutes using a microwave-safe dish with cover. Let stand.

3 cups frozen baby peas
1 cup water
NOTE: *You can toss the peas into the sauce if you want, but we like the peas on the side.*

...when timer rings for pasta...

6. Rinse pasta under hot water in a colander. Let drain and return to pasta pot. Cover, **no heat**, and let stand.
Serve the pasta on a plate or pasta bowl with the sauce poured over top. Garnish with croutons, crumbled bacon and Parmesan cheese.
Warning...This pasta is addicting! It's so creamy you would swear there was heavy cream in it!

prepared smashed croutons
prepared crumbled bacon
Parmesan cheese, light, grated
  (optional but amazing)

Serves 4-6

DINNER IS READY IN 30 MINUTES

Equipment List:

Large stove-top pot
Large nonstick fry pan
Stove-top pot w/ steamer
  basket
Colander
Plate
Cutting board
Sharp meat knife
Stirring spoon
Serving spoon
Mallet
Measuring cups and spoons
Paper towel

Per serving:

Calories	500
Fat	13.8 g
Protein	32.7 g
Carbohydrate	60.8 g
Fiber	3.2 g
Sodium	442 mg

U.S. Food Exchanges:	Cdn. Food Choices:
3 1/2 Starch	4 Carb
4 Meat-lean	4 1/2 Meat/Alt
1/2 Fat	
1 Vegetable	

prep crew
- cut chicken
- brown chicken
- cook pasta
- cook peas

Stove-top

20
to
prep

Tomapplesauce Meatballs with Rice and Broccoli

Don't change yet! Take out equipment.

Take out ingredients.

1. Combine rice and water in a large microwave-safe pot with lid. Place a paper towel under the pot. **Microwave** at high 8 minutes, then medium 8 minutes.
   I always use a large pot when I microwave rice to avoid spilling, but just in case I put a paper towel underneath.

1 1/2 cups basmati or white rice
3 cups water
paper towel

2. Combine beef, garlic powder, onion powder and pepper in a mixing bowl.
   Form into meatballs. (approx 1")

1 1/2 lbs or 675 g ground beef, extra-lean
1 tsp garlic powder
1/2 tsp onion powder (can be onion salt)
1/4 tsp pepper

   Place meatballs in large nonstick electric or stove-top **fry pan** on medium heat, adding to pan as you form each meatball.
   Start by placing the meatballs on the outside of pan moving toward the center. Flip them to brown other side.
   Chop onion, then add to pan.

1/2 cup chopped onion (fresh or frozen)

   In the uncleaned bowl, combine applesauce, tomato soup, honey and chili paste. *(Use a clean bowl if not making sauce immediately after forming meatballs)*

1/2 cup applesauce, unsweetened
1 can tomato soup (10 fl oz or 284 mL)
1 Tbsp liquid honey
1/2 tsp Sambal Oelek (crushed chili paste)
 (add more if you like it hot)

   Once meatballs have browned on both sides, pour sauce over top. Stir to coat.
   Once sauce starts to boil, **reduce heat** to low and let simmer until rice is cooked and has rested for 5 minutes. (stir meatballs occasionally)

   ...while rice is resting...

3. Trim broccoli then rinse in colander or steamer basket. Place water in the bottom of a **stove-top** pot and bring to a full boil with the broccoli in the basket above. Cover and set timer for 3 minutes...
   ...or microwave at high using a microwave-safe dish with cover for 3 minutes. Let stand. Add butter if you must.

1 lb or 450 g broccoli florets (2 heads)
1 cup water

butter (optional)

Serves 4-6

DINNER IS READY IN 30 MINUTES

Equipment List:

Stove-top pot w/ steamer
  basket
Large nonstick electric or
  stove-top fry pan
Large microwave-safe pot
  w/ lid
Large mixing bowl
Colander
Cutting board
Sharp veggie knife
Stirring spoon
Can opener
Measuring cups and spoons
Paper towel

Per serving:

Calories	433
Fat	12.8 g
Protein	26.9 g
Carbohydrate	52.8 g
Fiber	2.2 g
Sodium	368 mg

U.S. Food Exchanges:	Cdn. Food Choices:
2 1/2 Starch	3 Carb
3 Meat-lean	4 Meat/Alt
1 Fruit	1/2 Other
1 Fat	

prep crew
- form meatballs
- chop onion
- make sauce
- cook rice
- cook broccoli

stove-top

20 to prep

Crunchy Orange Chicken with Potatoes and Spinach Salad

Don't change yet! Take out equipment.

Take out ingredients.

1. Preheat **oven** to 350° F.

2. Combine orange juice, brown sugar, honey and mustard in a large lasagna or cake pan. Stir using whisk.

   Unroll chicken thighs and place flat in the large lasagna or cake pan. *Squish them together if you need to.* Spoon all the sauce evenly over chicken pieces.
   Sprinkle with spices and corn flake crumbs.

   Bake in preheated **oven**.
   Set timer 50 minutes.

3. Wash potatoes, then add to a different oven-safe pan. Drizzle with olive oil and toss until potatoes are well coated. Sprinkle with spice. Place in **oven** beside chicken.

4. Rinse spinach leaves under cold water in salad spinner and spin dry. Place in salad bowl. Peel mandarins and break into wedges. Toss into greens. Set aside in **fridge**.

   Combine mayonnaise, yogurt and poppy seeds in a small bowl in that order. Stir to blend, using a whisk or a fork, until smooth.
   Set aside on table.

   ...when timer rings for chicken...
   Remove chicken and potatoes from oven.
   Dinner is ready.

   This has such an amazing aroma while it's cooking, that by the time you eat you feel like the journey was half the fun.

Sauce for Chicken
1/2 cup orange juice, unsweetened
2 Tbsp brown sugar
2 Tbsp liquid honey
1 Tbsp Dijon mustard

chicken thighs, boneless, skinless
  (1 3/4 lb or 800 g)

2 tsp curry powder
1/4 tsp pepper
1 tsp table blend seasoning, salt-free
1 cup corn flake crumbs
You can buy these already crushed in the coating mix section of your grocery store... or you can crumble them in your hand directly over the chicken in the pan.

20 baby potatoes (or cut up 4 large)
1 Tbsp olive oil, extra-virgin
1 tsp original, all purpose seasoning, salt-free

6 oz or 170 g prewashed baby spinach
2 mandarins or oranges

Healthy Poppyseed Dressing
1/4 cup mayonnaise, light
1/4 cup French vanilla yogurt, low-fat
1/4 tsp poppy seeds
You may want to whisk in a tiny bit of 1% milk if you like your dressing a bit runnier.

Oh yes...you may want to add a few croutons to your salad like we do.

Serves 4-6

DINNER IS READY IN 60 MINUTES

Equipment List:

Large lasagna or cake pan
Medium oven-safe pan
Small mixing bowl
Cutting board
Salad spinner
Salad bowl
Salad tongs
Sharp veggie knife
Whisk
Stirring spoon
Fork
Measuring cups and spoons

Per serving:

Calories	468
Fat	11.6 g
Protein	32.4 g
Carbohydrate	61.0 g
Fiber	5.9 g
Sodium	367 mg

U.S. Food Exchanges:	Cdn. Food Choices:
3 Starch	4 Carb
4 Meat-lean	4 Meat/Alt
1 Fruit	
1/2 Fat	

prep crew

- assemble
- no cutting or chopping

Oven

15 to prep

Tuna Tetrazzini with Corn & Peas

Don't change yet! Take out equipment.	**Take out ingredients.**

1. Fill a large **stove-top** pot with water and bring to a boil, on high heat, for pasta.

water

2. Preheat **oven** to 350°F.

   Heat oil in a large nonstick electric or stove-top fry pan at medium heat. Finely chop onion and slice celery, adding to pan as you cut. Sauté until onion is soft and slightly browned. **Remove from heat**.

1 tsp olive oil
1/2 onion
2 celery ribs

3. Add pasta to boiling water and stir. Set timer for 8 minutes (or 2 minutes less than package directions.) When timer rings for pasta, rinse under cold water in a colander to remove starch. Return to pasta pot. **No heat.**

4 cups fusilli pasta
 (any kind of spiral pasta will do)

4. Add mushroom soup to cooked pasta. Add sautéed onion and celery.
   Crumble drained tuna into pasta pot using a fork. Add the first batch of cheese.
   Gradually stir in milk until all ingredients are well combined then transfer to an oven proof casserole dish. **(It may seem like there is too much liquid, but don't worry it will all dissappear once it's baked.)**

1 can cream of mushroom soup,
 reduced-sodium (10 fl oz or 284 mL)
sauteed onion and celery
1 can solid tuna in water, drained
 (6 1/2 oz or 180 g)
1/2 cup Tex-Mex cheese, shredded
1 soup can, filled with 1% milk
 (1 1/4 cups)

   Pile the final layer of cheese on top and evenly spread it around. Cover tightly with foil.

1 cup Tex-Mex cheese, shredded
aluminum foil

   Place in hot **oven**. Set timer for 25 minutes.

5. Rinse peas and corn in a colander.
   Place in a microwave-safe pot or casserole with lid. **Microwave** at high for 4 minutes. Add butter, if you must.

2 cups frozen baby peas
2 cups frozen corn
 (peaches & cream style if available)
1 tsp butter (optional)

6. When timer rings for casserole you can **broil** the top to make the cheese crunchy. Set timer for 1-2 minutes so you don't forget it's under the broiler. *Believe me, the timer has saved me from a burnt mess many times!*

<u>**Serves 4-6**</u>

Equipment List:

Large nonstick electric or
  stove-top fry pan
Large stove-top pot
Large casserole dish w/ lid
Microwave-safe pot w/ lid
Cutting board
Colander
Can opener
Sharp veggie knife
Mixing spoon
Measuring cups and spoons
Aluminum foil

Per serving:

Calories	403
Fat	11.0 g
Protein	23.7 g
Carbohydrate	54.0 g
Fiber	4.9 g
Sodium	713 mg

U.S. Food Exchanges:	Cdn. Food Choices:
3 Starch	3 1/2 Carb
2 Meat-lean	3 Meat/Alt
1 Vegetable	1/2 Fat
1 Fat	

prep crew
- cut onion
- cut celery
- assemble
- cook peas
  and corn
- cook pasta
stove-top/oven

TAKE 5

15
to
prep

About The Recipes

Maple Cranberry Chicken Breasts

I love to experiment with different flavors. Tossing things like dried cranberries into recipes can add such an unusual touch to both flavor and appearance. This is such an easy recipe to prepare. A great entertaining dish, too. It will look like you fussed for hours!

Macaroni Lasagna

This is the junk food meal of the week. Kids go nuts over this. It really has a delicious flavor. If you are vegetarian, veggie grind works great!

Chicken & Mushrooms in Pastry

This recipe is fabulous, easy and very gourmet. Most of our test families rated it 10 for weekday cooking. This is a great recipe to have in your back pocket after Thanksgiving or Christmas because it works great with turkey.

Take 5 - You can cut up your chicken and veggies the night before.

We tested this with mixed mushrooms for a vegetarian dish and found it absolutely amazing.

Chicken Tortellini Soup

I don't know what it is with me and tortellini in soup, but it's just one of those things that turns soup into a filling, stick to the ribs meal for me! For a spicier version add more hot sauce or spice. Vegetarians, you can leave out the chicken and add mixed beans or pressed tofu. The reason I always put my pasta in the bottom of the bowl instead of right into the soup is so it doesn't get mushy, especially by the next day! Just pour hot soup over the noodles and it's always perfect.

Oven Pork Roast

This is honestly one of the most delicious pork roasts you will ever eat.

We completely revamped this recipe. We tested and tested six times in total, not counting our test families. We think it's now foolproof for roasts between 2-4 pounds.

Maple Cranberry Chicken Breasts with Rice and Broccoli

Our Family Rating: 9

Your Family Rating: _____

Macaroni Lasagna with Veggies & Dip

Our Family Rating: 9

Your Family Rating: _____

Chicken & Mushrooms in Pastry with Pesto Glazed Veggies

Our Family Rating: 9

Your Family Rating: _____

TAKE

Chicken Tortellini Soup

Our Family Rating: 10

Your Family Rating: _____

TAKE

Oven Pork Roast with Applesauce, Baby Potatoes, Gravy & Asparagus

Our Family Rating: 9.5

Your Family Rating: _____

Blue

Yellow

Blue

Yellow

Green

Maple Cranberry Chicken Breasts with Rice and Broccoli

Don't change yet! Take out equipment.

Take out ingredients.
<u>Flour Coating For Chicken</u>
2 tsp butter
2 tsp prepared garlic (from a jar)
waxed paper
1/4 cup flour
1/8 tsp salt
1/8 tsp pepper
1/8 tsp rosemary leaves

1. Melt butter in a nonstick electric or stove-top **fry pan** on medium-low heat. Add garlic. Combine flour, salt, pepper and rosemary on a large piece of waxed paper.

   Coat the chicken in flour mixture and brown in pan on both sides.
   Cut green onion and slice mushrooms.
   Add to pan as you cut.
   …meanwhile…
   Combine maple syrup, vinegar and water in a small bowl.
   Pour over chicken once chicken is browned.
   Sprinkle cranberries around chicken pieces.
   Reduce heat slightly for a high simmer. Set timer for 20 minutes. (Check the chicken frequently to make sure the liquid isn't evaporating too much. Add a little water at a time if it is. You want it a little saucy.)

4 chicken breasts, boneless skinless (1 1/2 lbs or 675 g)
3 green onions
10 mushrooms
<u>Maple-Cranberry Sauce for Chicken</u>
1/2 cup maple syrup
2 Tbsp apple cider vinegar
2 Tbsp water
1/4 cup dried cranberries, unsweetened

2. Combine rice and water in a large microwave-safe pot. Place a paper towel under the pot. Cover, **no heat** and leave in microwave until timer rings for chicken.
   ...when timer rings for chicken...
   Reduce heat for chicken to a low simmer.

   Microwave rice at high 8 minutes, then medium 8 minutes.

1 1/4 cups basmati or white rice
2 1/2 cups water
paper towel

   ...meanwhile...

3. Trim broccoli then rinse in colander or steamer basket. Place water in the bottom of a **stove-top** pot and bring to a full boil with the broccoli in the basket above. Cover and set timer for 3 minutes...
   ...or microwave at high using a microwave-safe dish with cover for 3 minutes. Let stand. Toss with spice and butter if you wish.

1 lb or 450 g broccoli florets (2 heads)
1 cup water

1/2 tsp table blend seasoning, salt-free
butter (optional)
<u>Serves 4-6</u>

DINNER IS READY IN 60 MINUTES

Equipment List:

Large nonstick electric or
stove-top fry pan
Large microwave-safe pot
w/ lid
Stove-top pot w/ steamer
basket
Colander
Cutting board
Small mixing bowl
Mixing bowl or plastic bag
Sharp veggie knife
Measuring cups and spoons
Paper towel
Waxed paper.

Per serving:

Calories	475
Fat	4.0 g
Protein	32.5 g
Carbohydrate	77.5 g
Fiber	3.2 g
Sodium	157 mg

U.S. Food Exchanges:	Cdn. Food Choices:
4 Starch	4 Carb
3 1/2 Meat-lean	4 Meat/Alt
1 Other Carb	1 Other

prep crew
- coat chicken breasts
- make sauce
- cook chicken
- cook rice
- cook broccoli

Stove-top/
microwave

20
to
prep

2

Macaroni Lasagna with Veggies & Dip

Don't change yet! Take out equipment.

Take out ingredients.

1. Preheat **oven** to 375º F.

2. Fill a large **stove-top** pot with water and bring to boil for pasta.

   water

3. Brown meat in a large nonstick electric or stove-top **fry pan** at med-high until meat is no longer pink. Add onion flakes and spice while meat is browning.

   1 lb or 450 g ground beef, extra-lean
   1 Tbsp onion flakes
   1 tsp Italian seasoning
   1 tsp hot chili flakes (optional)

4. Place macaroni in boiling water and stir. Set timer for 5 minutes. (or 2 minutes less than package directions)

   2 1/2 cups macaroni, whole wheat

   …meanwhile…

5. Mix together mayonnaise, sour cream and spice in a small mixing bowl to make veggie dip. Let stand in **fridge**.

   <u>Light Veggie Dip</u>
   1/2 cup mayonnaise, light
   1/2 cup sour cream, fat-free or light
   1/2 tsp garlic and herb seasoning, salt-free

   Rinse veggies and arrange on a serving plate.

   1 1/2 lbs or 675 g precut veggies
      (approx 6 cups celery, cauliflower, broccoli and carrots)

   ...when timer rings for pasta...

6. Rinse pasta in colander and let drain.

7. Layer ingredients into a large lasagna or cake pan in this order: 1/2 of the fully cooked beef, 1/2 of the cooked macaroni, 1/2 pasta sauce and 1/2 cheese. Repeat.

   prepared cooked beef
   prepared cooked macaroni
   1 can tomato pasta sauce
      (24 fl oz or 680 mL)
      (choose a lower sodium brand)
      I use a spicy blend.

   Bake uncovered in **preheated oven**.
   Set timer for 20 minutes or until top layer of cheese is bubbly.

   2 cups cheddar cheese, light, shredded

   Set the table…and dinner is served!

   <u>Serves 6-8</u>

DINNER IS READY IN 30 MINUTES

Equipment List:

Large nonstick electric or
   stove-top fry pan
Large stove-top pot
Large lasagna or cake pan
Colander
Small mixing bowl
Serving plate
Small stirring spoon
2 large stirring spoons
Measuring cups and spoons

Per serving:

Calories	426
Fat	17.4 g
Protein	25.5 g
Carbohydrate	42.4 g
Fiber	6.4 g
Sodium	617 mg

U.S. Food Exchanges:	Cdn. Food Choices:
2 Starch	2 1/2 Carb
3 Meat-lean	3 Meat/Alt
2 Vegetable	1 1/2 Fat
2 Fat	

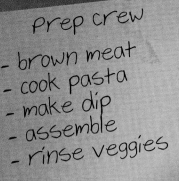

prep crew
- brown meat
- cook pasta
- make dip
- assemble
- rinse veggies

stove-top/oven

20 to prep

2

Chicken & Mushrooms in Pastry with Pesto Glazed Veggies

Don't change yet! Take out equipment.

Take out ingredients.

1. Preheat **oven** to **400° F.**

2. Melt butter in a medium **stove-top** pot on low heat. Wash and slice mushrooms adding to pot as you cut. Stir and **remove from heat**.

   2 Tbsp butter
   10 mushrooms

   Sprinkle flour into pot. Stir until mushrooms are coated. Gradually stir in chicken broth and milk. Stir in spice and Worcestershire sauce.

   2 Tbsp flour
   1 cup chicken broth, reduced-sodium
   1 cup 1% milk
   1/4 tsp black pepper
   1 tsp Italian seasoning
   1 tsp Worcestershire sauce

   Remove meat from roaster chicken and cut into cubes. Add to sauce. Fold in peas. Let stand, **no heat.**

   2 cups cooked roaster chicken (from a deli) (save the rest of the chicken for Chicken Tortellini Soup)
   1 cup frozen peas

   …meanwhile…

3. Place pastry shells on a cookie sheet and bake in preheated **oven**. Set timer for 20 minutes.

   1 pkg of 6 frozen puff pastry patti shells (10 oz or 300 g) *I like Tenderflake brand.* (can use precooked pastry shells found in bakery section in some stores)

4. Spray a large nonstick electric or stove-top **fry pan** with cooking spray and heat at medium. Rinse peppers and zucchini and cut into large chunks adding to pan as you cut. Dab with pesto and toss. Cook until tender.

   cooking spray
   1 red bell pepper
   1 yellow bell pepper
   2 medium zucchini
   1 Tbsp basil pesto

5. **Reheat** sauce on medium until it starts to thicken.

   ...when timer rings for pastry...

6. Remove from **oven**. Remove top center disk using a fork and set aside. Gently lift out the soft pastry from the inside of the shell and discard, leaving the bottom intact.

   When you are ready to serve, place a shell on each plate and fill with sauce. Put a pastry disk on top of the sauce. Serve alongside veggies.

   Serves 4-6

YUUUUUUUMMMY…and it looks amazing, so it's also a great entertaining dish.

DINNER IS READY IN 40 MINUTES

Equipment List:

Medium stove-top pot
Large nonstick electric or
   stove-top fry pan
Cookie sheet
2 cutting boards
Stirring spoon
Can opener
Whisk
Flipper
Sharp meat knife
Sharp veggie knife
Fork
Measuring cups and spoons

Per serving:

Calories	396
Fat	21.2 g
Protein	21.0 g
Carbohydrate	31.1 g
Fiber	2.9 g
Sodium	364 mg

U.S. Food Exchanges:	Cdn. Food Choices:
2 Starch	2 Carb
3 Meat-lean	3 Meat/Alt
2 Fat	2 Fat

prep crew
- cut mushrooms
- cook sauce
- remove chicken
  & cube
- bake patti shells
- saute veggies
- cut veggies
stove-top/
oven

2

TAKE 5

20 to prep

Chicken Tortellini Soup

Don't change yet! Take out equipment.

Take out ingredients.

1. Fill a large **stove-top** pot with water and bring to a boil for pasta.

water

2. Heat oil in a different large **stove-top** pot at medium. Sliver onion, adding to pot as you cut. Cut celery and carrots into chunks, adding to pot as you cut.
Cut chicken into bite size pieces, adding to pot as you cut.

Add broth, water, spice, Worcestershire sauce and hot sauce to pot. **Reduce heat** to simmer.

1 tsp olive oil, extra-virgin
1 onion
2 celery ribs
2 carrots
2 cups cooked roaster chicken (from a deli) or use leftover chicken or pork or sauté cut up chicken breast
3 1/2 - 4 cups chicken broth, reduced-sodium
2 1/2 cups water
1/4 tsp celery salt
1/4 tsp poultry seasoning
1/4 tsp fresh ground pepper
1 tsp garlic and herb seasoning, salt-free
1 tsp Worcestershire sauce
1 tsp hot sauce (optional)

Add peas to up the veggies, or serve with a salad kit.

1 cup frozen peas (optional)
salad kit (optional)

3. Place pasta in boiling water. Stir and set timer according to package directions, approx 8 minutes.

4 cups cheese tortellini (12 oz or 350 g) (found in deli or dairy section)

…when timer rings for pasta…
Rinse pasta in colander and let drain.

...when carrots pierce easily with a fork...
Place tortellini in the bottom of your bowl and ladle hot soup over top.

<u>Serves 6</u>

DINNER IS READY IN 25 MINUTES

Equipment List:

2 large stove-top pots
2 cutting boards
Colander
Ladle
Sharp veggie knife
Sharp meat knife
Fork
Measuring cups and spoons

Per serving:

Calories	340
Fat	9.3 g
Protein	24.0 g
Carbohydrate	40.3 g
Fiber	2.7 g
Sodium	712 mg

U.S. Food Exchanges:	Cdn. Food Choices:
2 1/2 Starch	2 1/2 Carb
3 Meat	3 Meat/Alt
1 Vegetable	

prep crew
- cut veggies
- saute veggies
- cook pasta
- remove and
  cut chicken
- simmer soup

Stove-top

2

TAKE 5

20
to
prep

Oven Pork Roast with Applesauce, Baby Potatoes, Gravy and Asparagus

Take out equipment.

Take out ingredients.

1. Preheat **oven** to **500° F**

2. Place roast on oven-safe metal pan. Evenly sprinkle spice over top. Let stand.
   IMPORTANT: Save meat wrapper to calculate the exact weight of your roast.

   2 lbs or 900 g pork loin roast, boneless, trimmed (approx)
   1/2 tsp fresh ground pepper
   1 tsp garlic powder
   1 tsp original, all purpose seasoning, salt-free

   ...meanwhile...

3. Rinse potatoes and place in a different oven safe metal pan. Drizzle with oil and toss to coat. Sprinkle with spice.

   20 baby potatoes (or 4 large thin skinned potatoes cut into pieces)
   1 tsp canola oil
   1/2 tsp rosemary leaves

4. Place roast and potatoes in preheated **oven**, beside each other, uncovered. Set timer for 24 minutes (**12 min per lb, see meat wrapper**).
   …when timer rings for roast…
   IMPORTANT: **Turn oven off but do not open oven door! Leave roast and potatoes in the oven!** Set timer for 30 minutes.

   If you have a larger roast, take potatoes out of oven after 24 minutes, then return them to oven for 30 minutes once it's turned off.

   …meanwhile…
   Whisk together gravy mix and water in a small **stove-top** pot. Whisk in the extra water.
   Bring to a boil on high heat, stirring continuously. **Remove from heat.**

   <u>Gravy Mix</u>
   3 Tbsp dry brown gravy mix *I like Bisto.*
   combined with
   3 Tbsp water
   1 1/2 cups water (add more if needed)

5. Snap off bottom nodes of asparagus and discard. *See page 35.* Rinse in colander or steamer basket. Place water in the bottom of a **stove-top** pot and let stand. **No heat.**
   Combine applesauce and cinnamon in a small serving bowl. Set aside to serve with the roast.

   20 asparagus spears

   1 cup water

   1/2 cup applesauce, unsweetened
   pinch of cinnamon (*Leave applesauce out if you only want gravy.*)

   ...when timer rings for roast...

6. Internal temperature should be 150º F (moister) or leave in a little longer for 160º F (drier). Transfer roast to plate. Wrap in foil to rest. **Reheat gravy.** Whisk in juices from the resting roast into gravy.

   You may need to leave the roast in for a little longer depending on your oven.
   aluminum foil
   reserved gravy

7. Bring asparagus water to a full boil with the asparagus in the basket above. Cover and set timer for 4 minutes...
   ...or microwave for the 4 minutes.

   An oven thermometer only costs a few bucks and it's a great thing to own to make sure your oven is cooking at the right temperature

   <u>Serves 4-6</u>

DINNER IS READY IN 60 MINUTES

Equipment List:

2 Oven-safe metal pans
Small stove-top pot
Stove-top pot w/ steamer
  basket
Large plate
Small serving bowl
Whisk
Spatula
Sharp meat knife
Instant-read thermometer
Measuring cups and spoons
Aluminum foil

Per serving:

Calories	370	
Fat	9.3	g
Protein	37.7	g
Carbohydrate	33.5	g
Fiber	4.9	g
Sodium	225	mg

U.S. Food Exchanges:	Cdn. Food Choices:
2 Starch	2 Carb
4 Meat-lean	4 Meat/Alt

prep crew
- spice roast & potatoes
- cook roast, potatoes and asparagus
- make gravy mix
- prep asparagus
- get applesauce ready

Stove-top/oven

15 to prep

2

About The Recipes

Beef & Broccoli

This has fantastic flavor.

Take 5 - Cutting up the veggies and/or the meat the night before can really help if your Cooking Together/Apart.

If you like it veggie version, firm tofu is fabulous with this!

Peanut Butter & Honey Chicken

Our test families love this meal recipe. It's all about the oven, so there's no cutting or chopping.

Spaghetti & Lean Meat Sauce

This is such a great spaghetti sauce and it freezes beautifully. Remember the recipe is designed to take some out right away, before you serve, to freeze for when you are making your Leftover Lasagna and Cheeseburger Soup.

For vegetarians, this dish is absolutely perfect with veggie grind.

Mediterranean Pizza and Cheese Pizza

When the kids were little they used to think our family was weird because we would make our own pizza. They wanted to be like other families who had their pizzas delivered. Ron and I would treat the kids and ourselves (no dishes) to the boxed variety occasionally. One day when I was about to order the family pizza, as a treat, they all rebelled. They had gotten used to the ones we made at home. The teens even offered (yes, I said offered) to drive to the store and get the ingredients!

Butter Chicken

I've tried 'em all! I keep trying to perfect this so it's easy and healthy. As you can appreciate, with a name like butter chicken...well, that wasn't exactly easy! I loooove this recipe. It's yummy, it's quick, it's gourmet, yet down home with a twist. OK, I'll shut up now!

Vegetarians, fry up some firm tofu and throw it in.

Beef & Broccoli with Rice

Our Family Rating: 10

Your Family Rating: _____

TAKE

Y e l l o w

Peanut Butter & Honey Chicken with Fries and Snap Peas

Our Family Rating: 10

Your Family Rating: _____

G r e e n

Spaghetti & Lean Meat Sauce with Veggies & Dip

Our Family Rating: 9

Your Family Rating: _____

Y e l l o w

Mediterranean Pizza and Cheese Pizza

Our Family Rating: 10

Your Family Rating: _____

TAKE

R e d

Butter Chicken with Basmati Rice and Baby Peas

Our Family Rating: 10

Your Family Rating: _____

Y e l l o w

Beef & Broccoli with Rice

Don't change yet! Take out equipment.

1. Combine rice and water in a large microwave-safe pot with lid. Place a paper towel under the pot. **Microwave** at high 8 minutes, then medium 8 minutes.

2. Heat oil in a large nonstick electric or stove-top **fry pan** or wok at med-high. Cut meat into thin strips against the grain and add to pan as you cut.
Toss occasionally.
Add garlic, pepper and dried chili flakes.

   Slice onion into thin strips and add to pan as you slice.
Rinse mushrooms, broccoli and zucchini.
Cut mushrooms in half or quarters adding to pan as you cut.
Trim and cut broccoli into bite size pieces adding to pan as you cut.
Slice zucchini in half, lengthwise, then into thirds. Slice each segment into long sticks.
Add to pan as you cut.

   Combine brown sugar, ginger, sweet soy sauce, peanut satay sauce and water. Pour over meat and veggies. Stir until well coated and continue to cook until broccoli is tender.

   ...when timer rings for rice...
3. Leave in microwave for about 5 minutes to set.
   ...then enjoy!!! Careful it's hot!

Take out ingredients.

1 1/2 cups basmati rice (or quinoa)
3 cups water
paper towel

1 tsp canola oil
1 1/2 lbs or 675 g flank or skirt steak, trimmed of fat (or lean sirloin steak)

1 Tbsp fresh garlic (from a jar)
2 tsp fresh ginger (from a jar)
1/2 tsp fresh ground pepper
1/4-1/2 tsp hot chili flakes (optional)
1 onion

10-12 fresh mushrooms
1 lb or 450 g broccoli florets (2 heads)
1 small zucchini

<u>Stir Fry Sauce</u>
1 Tbsp brown sugar
2 tsp fresh ginger (from a jar)
1 Tbsp sweet soy sauce, Kepac Manis
   (or 1 Tbsp dark soy sauce
   and 1 tsp honey)
1/4 cup peanut satay sauce
1/3-1/2 cup water

<u>Serves 4-6</u>

DINNER IS READY IN 30 MINUTES

Equipment List:

Large microwave-safe pot
  w/ lid
Large nonstick electric or
  stove-top fry pan or wok
Small mixing bowl
2 cutting boards
Sharp veggie knife
Sharp meat knife
2 stirring spoons
Measuring cups & spoons
Paper towel

Per serving:

Calories	425
Fat	11.1 g
Protein	32.7 g
Carbohydrate	49.5 g
Fiber	2.3 g
Sodium	158 mg

U.S. Food Exchanges:	Cdn. Food Choices:
3 Starch	3 Carb
3 Meat-lean	4 Meat/Alt
1/2 Fat	
1 Vegetable	

prep crew
- brown meat
- cook rice
- cut & cook veggies
- make sauce

stove-top/
microwave

TAKE 5

20 to prep

3

Peanut Butter & Honey Chicken with Fries and Snap Peas

Don't change yet! Take out equipment.

Take out ingredients.

1. Preheat **oven** to 425° F.

2. Soften peanut butter and honey in a small bowl for approx 10 seconds in the **microwave**. Whisk in soy sauce.

   2 Tbsp peanut butter, light
   2 Tbsp liquid honey
   2 tsp soy sauce, reduced-sodium
    (or use Bragg)

   Unroll chicken thighs and place flat in an oven-safe pan. Spread peanut butter and honey mixture evenly over chicken with the back of a spoon. Sprinkle with sesame seeds.

   10-12 chicken thighs, boneless, skinless
    (1 3/4 lbs or 800 g)

   2 Tbsp sesame seeds

   Place chicken in preheated **oven**. Set timer for 10 minutes to remind you to put the fries in. *Chicken actually cooks for 30-35 minutes or until internal temp is 170° F.*

   Always use an instant read thermometer to ensure the chicken is cooked through, they are only a few bucks and really help you to know when dinner is ready.

   …when timer rings for chicken...
3. Leave chicken in.
   Scatter fries on a cookie sheet with sides in a single layer and place in oven. Set timer for 10 minutes. When timer rings, remove fries from oven, flip fries and reset timer for an additional 10 minutes (or follow package directions.)

   1 lb or 450 g frozen sweet potato fries
    (or regular fries)
   Look for the least ingredients and no trans fats.

   …meanwhile…
4. Rinse snap peas in a colander. Add to a large nonstick electric or stove-top **fry pan**. Let stand.

   1 lb or 450 g snap peas

   1/2 tsp sesame oil

   ...when timer rings for chicken and fries...
   Turn heat to high for snap peas. Drizzle with sesame oil and toss until hot and fragrant.
   If you want to skip sautéing them serve them fresh. They are great just as they are!

   <u>**Serves 4-6**</u>

DINNER IS READY IN 55 MINUTES

Equipment List:

Oven-safe pan
Large nonstick electric or
   stove-top fry pan
Cookie sheet w/ sides
Colander
Small microwave-safe
   mixing bowl
Flipper
Whisk
Stirring spoon
Spoon
Instant read thermometer
Measuring cups and spoons

Per serving:

Calories	393
Fat	14.4 g
Protein	31.0 g
Carbohydrate	34.7 g
Fiber	6.2 g
Sodium	357 mg

U.S. Food Exchanges:	Cdn. Food Choices:
1 Starch	1 Carb
4 Meat	4 Meat/Alt
1 Vegetable	1/2 Fat
1/2 Other	1 Other

prep crew
- prep chicken
- get fries on pan
- bake chicken & fries
- rinse snap peas
- cook snap peas
- no cutting & chopping

stove-top/oven

15
to
prep

Spaghetti and Lean Meat Sauce with Veggies & Dip

Don't change yet! Take out equipment.

1. Fill a large **stove-top pot** with water and bring to a boil for pasta.

2. Brown meat at med-high in a second large **stove-top** pot until meat is no longer pink. Chop onion and bell pepper (finely). Add to meat as you chop and stir. Add garlic and pepper. Rinse and slice mushrooms. Add to pot as you slice.
   Add sauce to cooked meat and stir. **Reduce heat** and simmer for 15 minutes. Swish water into each can to remove the sauce from sides of can and add to the sauce.

   NOTE: *This is fabulous in the slow cooker as it simmers all day long with no extra work.*

3. Place pasta in boiling water and stir. Set timer according to package directions, approx 8 minutes.

   ...while pasta is cooking...
4. Rinse veggies.
   Cut celery into large pieces and sliver pepper.
   Arrange on a plate.
   Serve with dip.

   ...when timer rings for pasta...
5. Rinse pasta in a colander under hot water. Return to pot. *I like to toss the pasta with a little olive oil and basil.*

   Parmesan and chili flakes are a nice touch!

   BEFORE YOU SERVE
   Set aside 4 cups sauce for the French Loaf Lasagnas and 3 cups for Cheeseburger Soup... then you'll be one step ahead next week. You will have 5 cups left for this dinner.

   The meat sauce freezes beautifully.

Take out ingredients.

water
SAUCE FOR 4 DINNERS
(Extra sauce is for 3 meals in Week 4 French Loaf x 2 and Cheeseburger Soup)

1 1/2 lb or 675 g ground beef, extra-lean
1 large onion
1/2 green or red bell pepper or 1 small
1 Tbsp prepard garlic
1/2 tsp fresh ground pepper
12 mushrooms
3 cans tomato pasta sauce, Spicy Onion & Garlic or your favorite
  (24 fl oz or 680 mL each can)
  (choose a lower sodium brand)
1 cup water (1/3 cup per can)

12 oz or 340 g spaghetti pasta

2 cups snap peas
2 celery ribs
1 red, orange or yellow bell pepper
12 grape tomatoes
cauliflower and cucumber (optional)
1/4 cup salad dressing, ranch, light or your favorite (choose a lower sodium brand)

1 tsp olive oil, extra-virgin
1 tsp basil (optional)

Parmesan (optional)
hot chili flakes (optional)

Serves 4-6

DINNER IS READY IN 30 MINUTES

Equipment List:

Large stove-top pot
Second large stove-top pot
   (or large fry-pan and
   slow cooker)
Colander
Cutting board
Serving plate
Sharp veggie knife
Large stirring spoon
Pasta fork
Can opener
Serving plate
Measuring cups & spoons

Per serving:

Calories	434
Fat	10.3 g
Protein	20.2 g
Carbohydrate	64.5 g
Fiber	7.0 g
Sodium	538 mg

U.S. Food Exchanges:	Cdn. Food Choices:
3 1/2 Starch	4 Carb
2 Meat-lean	3 Meat/Alt
1 Fat	1/2 Fat
1 Vegetable	

Assumes 7 cups sauce reserved and 5 cups eaten.

Prep crew
- brown meat
- cut veggies
- cook pasta and sauce
- set aside sauce
  for Cheeseburger Soup
  & French Loaf Lasagna

Stove-top

20 to prep

3

Mediterranean Pizza and Cheese Pizza

Don't change yet! Take out equipment.

Take out ingredients.

1. Preheat **oven** to 375°F.

First Pizza

2. Combine olive oil, garlic and spices in a small cup to make a spiced oil base.

Brush oil base evenly over one pizza crust, but only when you are ready to make the pizza.

Mediterranean Pizza Oil Base
1 1/2 Tbsp olive oil
1 tsp fresh garlic (from a jar)
1/8 tsp dried basil
1/8 tsp thyme leaves
1/8 tsp rosemary
1/8 tsp oregano
1 thin-crust pizza crust, 12"

Rinse and layer over pizza as you slice zucchini, mushrooms and peppers.

Toppings for Mediterranean Pizza
1/3 of a small zucchini
3-5 mushrooms
1/2 red, yellow or orange bell pepper
  (cut extra veggies and set aside for people choosing cheese pizza)
1/8 red onion
3 artichoke hearts (from a can)
  (the balance can be frozen)
6-8 sundried tomatoes
sliced olives (optional)

Sliver red onion, artichokes and sundried tomatoes, layering over pizza as you cut.

Scatter feta evenly all over and top with shredded mozzarella. Scatter pine nuts over cheese.

1/4 cup feta cheese, light
1/2 cup mozzarella cheese, part skim, shredded
1 Tbsp pine nuts or matchstick almonds

Second Pizza

3. Brush a thin layer of oil all over crust.
   (it helps the crust not to get soggy)
Spread sauce evenly over crust with the back of a spoon.
Sprinkle with spice.
Cover with shredded cheese.

Regular Cheese Pizza
2 tsp olive oil
1 thin-crust pizza crust, 12"
1/4 cup pizza sauce (from a can)
1 tsp Italian seasoning
lean pepperoni (optional)
1 cup mozzarella cheese, part skim, shredded

Bake in preheated **oven** on separate middle racks at opposite sides of oven.
Set timer for 8-10 minutes.
...when timer rings...
You may want to bubble up the cheese on **broil**. WATCH CAREFULLY OR YOU'LL HAVE A BURNT MESS, AND YOU'LL CRY!

Serves 6

DINNER IS READY IN 30 MINUTES

Equipment List:

Cutting board
Pastry brush
Sharp veggie knife
Cheese grater
Liquid measuring cup
Measuring cups and spoons

Per serving:

Calories	389
Fat	15.4 g
Protein	17.0 g
Carbohydrate	49.3 g
Fiber	6.6 g
Sodium	851 mg

U.S. Food Exchanges:	Cdn. Food Choices:
3 Starch	3 Carb
1 1/2 Meat	2 1/2 Meat/Alt
2 Fat	1 1/2 Fat

prep crew

- prep spiced oil
- cut veggies
- assemble

Oven

TAKE 5

15 to prep

3

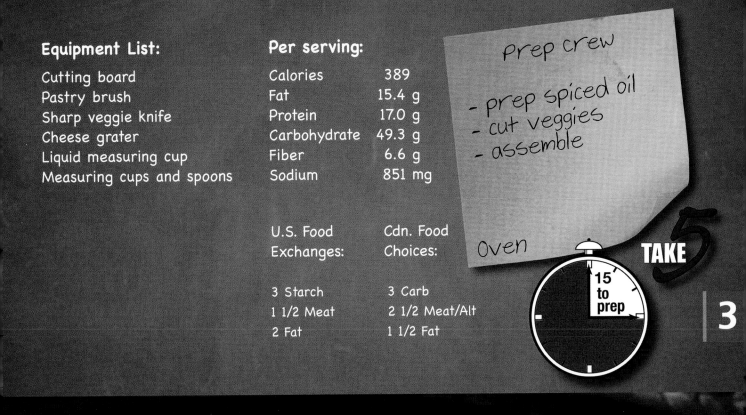

Butter Chicken with Basmati Rice and Baby Peas

Take out equipment.

Take out ingredients.

1. Melt butter in a large **stove-top** pot at med-high heat.

   1/4 cup butter

   Cut each breast into bite size chunks, adding to butter as you cut. Toss until no longer pink. **Remove from heat.**

   4 chicken breasts, boneless, skinless (1 1/3 lbs or 600 g) or 8-10 chicken thighs

   Add garam masala, paprika, cinnamon, sugar, chili powder, Madras curry and peanut butter. Stir to coat.

   1 Tbsp garam masala (spice blend)
   1 tsp paprika
   1 tsp cinnamon
   1 tsp sugar
   1/2 tsp chili powder
   1 Tbsp Madras curry paste
   1 Tbsp peanut butter, light

   Gradually stir in tomato soup, cream, milk and chicken broth. Chop cilantro and toss into pot. Return to medium-low heat and stir. (You want a high simmer.)

   1 can tomato soup (10 fl oz or 284 mL)
   1/2 of the soup can, filled with 10% cream
   1/2 of the soup can, filled with 1% milk
   3/4 cup chicken broth, reduced-sodium
   1/4 cup fresh cilantro (optional *but amazing*)

2. Combine rice and water in a large microwave-safe pot with lid. Place a paper towel under the pot. **Microwave** at high for 8 minutes, then medium for 8 minutes.

   1 1/2 cups basmati rice
   3 cups water
   paper towel
   A few whole cloves are a nice option to throw into the rice while it's cooking.

   ...when timer rings for rice, leave in microwave...

3. Rinse peas in colander or steamer basket. Place water in the bottom of a **stove-top** pot and bring to a full boil with the peas in the basket above. Cover and set timer for 3 minutes...
   ... on high for 3-4 minutes using a microwave-safe dish with cover. Let stand.

   3 cups frozen baby peas (or leftover fresh veggies)
   1 cup water

   If you've never had butter chicken, there's LOTS of sauce, so don't be surprised... that's the way it's supposed to be. Adding naan bread to this meal makes it extra special for entertaining!

   naan bread (optional) *Nann bread is easy to find in most bakery sections.*

   <u>Serves 4-6</u>

DINNER IS READY IN 30 MINUTES

Equipment List:

Large stove-top pot
Large microwave-safe pot
  w/ lid
Stove-top pot
  w/ steamer basket
Colander
Cutting board
Sharp meat knife
Can opener
Mixing spoon
Measuring cups and spoons
Paper towel

Per serving:

Calories	519
Fat	18.5 g
Protein	30.7 g
Carbohydrate	58.0 g
Fiber	5.8 g
Sodium	630 mg

U.S. Food Exchanges:	Cdn. Food Choices:
3 Starch	3 1/2 Carb
2 1/2 Meat-lean	2 1/2 Meat/Alt
2 Fat	2 Fat
1/2 Milk-low fat	

prep crew
- cut chicken
- cook chicken
  & sauce
- cook rice
- cook peas

stove-top

20 to prep

3

About The Recipes

French Loaf Lasagna

Lasagna in the work week is a pain in the butt. This is not only easier the night you make it, but also provides you with an emergency back up meal...oh yea!
Vegetarians, use veggie grind.

Dijon Baked Chicken

Okay, reeeeeeeeeeeeeally good! I just love this meal! I'm often asked if a person can just go ahead and replace chicken thighs with chicken breast. I choose thighs for certain meals because I love how moist they are with the sauce. The nutritional data is still excellent. Many people prefer to use breast. Go right ahead. Same great flavor, the meat's just not as moist!

Cheeseburger Soup

A Night Before recipe. One of my favorite soups! So hearty, so fun and sooo delicious!
This slow cooker meal can be left on low heat for up to 10 hours.
Vegetarians...we had to sauté the veggie grind so you can't have little cheeseburgers...but the flavor is still AMAZING!

Easy Fettuccini Carbonara

Our carbonara procedure is different than most. I avoid mixing the sauce and pasta together. Our test families confirmed that the usual method can screw up easily, because it's one of those meals that has to be served immediately. With kids, that's just ridiculous. By serving the sauce over the noodles, it buys you some flexibility.
Vegetarians, use veggie bacon.

The Crunchiest Ever Baked Chicken Fingers

When the test families got their hands on this recipe, they couldn't believe they ever bought boxed. Check out the nutritional data on this meal! It's like you're eating junk food when you're not! Note: Don't over cook your chicken or it gets dry! Take 5 - for the veggies.
<u>Curry Dip for Chicken Fingers:</u>
Combine 1/4 cup light sour cream and 1/4 cup light mayonnaise with 1/2 tsp curry powder.

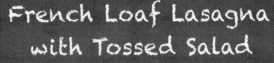

On The Menu - Week Four

French Loaf Lasagna
with Tossed Salad

Our Family Rating: 10

Your Family Rating: _____

Yellow

Dijon Baked Chicken
with Rice and Broccoli

Our Family Rating: 9.5

Your Family Rating: _____

Green

Cheeseburger Soup

Our Family Rating: 10

Your Family Rating: _____

Red

Easy Fettuccini Carbonara
with Almond Green Beans

Our Family Rating: 9.5

Your Family Rating: _____

Yellow

The Crunchiest Ever Baked
Chicken Fingers with Focaccia

Our Family Rating: 9.5

Your Family Rating: _____

TAKE

Red

French Loaf Lasagna with Tossed Salad

Don't change yet! Take out equipment.

1. Preheat **oven** to 425° F.

2. Slice bread lengthwise down the side to create two flat sides. Remove most of the white bread from the center of each side of the loaf with your fingers. Set aside in a bowl or discard (*I let the bread dry out in a bowl on the counter to make fine breadcrumbs*)

3. Smear sauce evenly over the bottom of each hollowed side.

   Dab cottage cheese evenly over sauce. Sprinkle with Parmesan cheese and top with mozzarella.

   Repeat layering.

   Place one of the halves, cheese side up, on a cookie sheet. Place in **preheated oven**. Set timer for 15 minutes.
   Depending on your oven you may have to bake it for an extra few minutes, to make sure the center is heated through.
   Wrap the other side in foil, then plastic and freeze for an emergency dinner another time.

   …while Lasagna Loaf is cooking…
4. Rinse spinach in salad spinner.
   Sliver red onion. Wash and sliver pepper.
   Divide spinach on serving plates and top with red onion, red pepper, blueberries and almonds.

   Drizzle with your favorite dressing.

   Brown the top of the loaf at **broil** if you like your cheese crunchier.
   Slice the Lasagna Loaf into thick slices and serve alongside the salad.

   This is a fork and knife meal, hard to pick up, just like lasagna.

Take out ingredients.
Use 4 cups reserved pasta sauce from Spaghetti dinner, page 68, or use canned.

1 loaf crusty French bread (we like using Calabrese, but it's not always easy to find)

First Layer
1 cup reserved pasta sauce, per side
(you can use the 4 cups reserved from Spaghetti dinner, page 70 or use canned)
1/2 cup 1% cottage cheese, per side
2 Tbsp Parmesan cheese, light, grated, per side
1/2 cup mozzarella, part-skim, shredded, per side

Second Layer
1 cup pasta sauce, per side
1/2 cup 1% cottage cheese, per side
2 Tbsp Parmesan cheese, light, grated, per side
1/2 cup mozzarella, part-skim, shredded, per side

aluminum foil
plastic wrap

6 oz or 170 g prewashed baby spinach
1/8 red onion
1/2 red bell pepper
1/4 cup wild blueberries, frozen
2 Tbsp matchstick almonds

3 Tbsp salad dressing, fruit vinaigrette, light, or your favorite
(choose a lower sodium brand)

Serves 4

DINNER IS READY IN 30 MINUTES

Equipment List:

Large stove-top pot
Cutting board
Salad spinner
Cheese grater
Sharp veggie knife
Bread knife
Salad tongs
Can opener
Stirring spoon
Spoon
Measuring cups and spoons
Aluminum foil
Plastic wrap

Per serving:

Calories	411
Fat	14.5 g
Protein	29.9 g
Carbohydrate	39.3 g
Fiber	5.5 g
Sodium	1096 mg

U.S. Food Exchanges:	Cdn. Food Choices:
2 Starch	2 1/2 Carb
4 Meat-lean	4 1/2 Meat/Alt
1/2 Fat	1/2 Fat
1/2 Fruit	

prep crew
- cut bread
- assemble
- rinse lettuce
- cut veggies for salad

Oven

20 to prep

One side of prepared French Loaf Lasagna is reserved for another meal. Assumes 1/3 of bread loaf removed.

Dijon Baked Chicken with Rice and Broccoli

Take out equipment.

Take out ingredients.

1. Preheat **oven** to 350° F

2. Combine rice and water in a large oven-safe pot. Stir. Cover and place in **oven.** (oven doesn't have to be fully preheated)

1 1/2 cups basmati or white rice
3 cups water

3. Combine the following in a large lasagna or cake pan in this order: spice, honey, Dijon mustard, soy sauce and chili paste. Stir using whisk.

Dijon Sauce for Chicken
1 Tbsp curry powder
1 Tbsp onion flakes
1/2 tsp hot chili flakes (optional)
1/2 cup liquid honey
1/2 cup Dijon mustard
2 Tbsp soy sauce, reduced-sodium
1 tsp Sambal Oelek (crushed chili paste)

Unroll chicken thighs and place flat in the large lasagna or cake pan. *Squish them together if you need to.*

10-12 chicken thighs, boneless, skinless
(1 3/4 lbs or 800 g)

Flip the chicken around with a fork until each piece is well coated. End by making sure the rough side of the chicken is down.

Place chicken in preheated **oven**, beside rice. Set timer for 40 minutes.

...when timer rings for chicken...
Turn oven off, but leave chicken and rice in the oven.

4. Trim broccoli then rinse in colander or steamer basket. Place water in the bottom of a **stove-top** pot and bring to a full boil with the broccoli in the basket above. Cover and set timer for 3 minutes...
...or microwave at high using a microwave-safe dish with cover for 3 minutes.

1 lb or 450 g broccoli florets (2 heads)
1 cup water

When timer rings toss with butter if you like and spice.

butter (optional)
1/4 tsp table blend seasoning, salt-free

Right before serving the chicken I flip it around in the pan with the Dijon sauce to glaze the tops.

<u>Serves 4-6</u>

DINNER IS READY IN 60 MINUTES

Equipment List:
Large lasagna or cake pan
Large oven-safe pot w/ lid
Stove-top pot
  w/ steamer basket
Colander
Whisk
Fork
Stirring spoon
Measuring cups and spoons

Per serving:

Calories	448
Fat	7.0 g
Protein	32.7 g
Carbohydrate	65.2 g
Fiber	2.1 g
Sodium	586 mg

U.S. Food Exchanges:	Cdn. Food Choices:
3 Starch	4 Carb
3 Meat v-lean	3 1/2 Meat/Alt
2 Vegetable	1/2 Other
1 Fat	
1/2 Other	

prep crew
- cook rice
- make sauce
- assemble
- trim & cook broccoli

Oven/microwave

15 to prep

Cheeseburger Soup

...night before...
Take out equipment.

Take out ingredients.
Use 3 cups reserved pasta sauce from
Spaghetti dinner, page 68, or use canned.

●▲

1. Heat oil in a large nonstick **fry pan** at
medium. *I use my electric fry pan for this.*
Sliver onion, adding to pan as you cut. Finely
chop celery, adding to pan as you cut. Sauté
until onion turns slightly brown.
Remove from heat.
Add to inside crock of **slow cooker.**

1 tsp olive oil, extra-virgin
1 onion
2 celery ribs

Reduce heat slightly of uncleaned fry pan.
Form tiny little pancake burgers (approx 1
1/2" in diameter and 1/4" thick) in the palm
of your hand and brown on both sides. Once
browned, add to **slow cooker**.

1 lb or 450 g ground beef, extra-lean

...while burgers are browning...
Add the following ingredients to **slow cooker**:
spice, bay leaves, stewed tomatoes,
consommé, water from both cans, pasta sauce
and mixed veggies. Stir to combine.

1 Tbsp Italian seasoning
1/4 tsp fresh ground pepper
1/4 tsp – 1/2 tsp hot chili flakes
 (optional for spice lovers)
3 bay leaves
1 can Italian or chili stewed tomatoes
 (14 fl oz or 400 mL)
1 tomato can filled with water
1 can consommé (10 fl oz or 284 mL)
1 consommé can filled with water
1 can tomato pasta sauce
 (24 fl oz or 680 mL each can)
 (choose a lower sodium brand)
 (You can use the 3 cups reserved from
 Spaghetti dinner, page 70.)
3 cups frozen mixed veggies

Refrigerate overnight.

...in the morning...

●▲

2. Set **slow cooker** at low heat. Simmer all day.

...when ready for dinner...

●▲

3. Serve with a bowl of grated cheddar cheese at
the table. Get the kids to lift their little burgers
to the top of the bowl so they can sprinkle
them with cheddar. *I actually find this fun!*

1/2 cup sharp cheddar cheese, light, grated

■

4. *Our family loves this with fresh buns, focaccia
or... I make extra pasta from the Carbonara
meal if making that earlier in the week. We
put a little pasta in the bottom of the bowl and
pour the soup over top. Either way it's a meal
in one and it is absolutely fun and delicious!!*

fresh buns or focaccia bread (optional)
leftover pasta (optional)

<u>Serves 6</u>

DINNER IS READY IN 30 MINUTES

Equipment List:

...the night before...
Slow cooker
Large nonstick electric or
  stove-top fry pan
Cutting board
Sharp veggie knife
Stirring spoon
Can opener
Measuring cups and spoons

...in the morning...
Slow cooker

...when ready for dinner...
Cheese grater
Cutting board
Bread knife
Ladle

Per serving:

Calories	416
Fat	12.6 g
Protein	28.7 g
Carbohydrate	50.2 g
Fiber	13.3 g
Sodium	959 mg

U.S. Food Exchanges:	Cdn. Food Choices:
1 1/2 Starch	1 1/2 Carb
4 Meat-lean	4 Meat/Alt
1 Vegetable	1 Other
1/2 Other	

prep crew
- cut and saute
  onion & celery
- prep little burgers
- cook little burgers
- assemble

Stove-top/
slowcooker

15
to
prep

Easy Fettuccini Carbonara with Almond Green Beans

Don't change yet! Take out equipment.

Take out ingredients.

1. Fill a large **stove-top** pot with water and bring to a boil for pasta.

water

Egg Mixture
3 egg yolks
1/2 cup 10% cream
1 1/4 cups 1% milk
1/2 cup Parmesan cheese, grated, light
1/2 tsp onion powder

2. Beat egg yolks lightly in a medium-size bowl. Whisk in cream, milk, Parmesan cheese and onion powder. Set aside.

3. Add pasta to boiling water then **reduce heat** to med-high. Stir to separate. Set timer according to package directions (approx 10 minutes).

3/4 lb or 340 g fettuccini pasta

...while pasta is cooking...

4. Heat olive oil in a different **stove-top** pot at medium heat. Cut bacon into chunks (or tear with hands) and add to pot. Slice green onion adding to pot as you cut. Stir. **Reduce heat** to low and let cook for 2 minutes. **Remove from heat,** then slowly whisk in egg mixture. **Return to heat** and continue to whisk occasionally while sauce simmers.

1 Tbsp olive oil, extra-virgin
8 strips fully cooked bacon, reduced-sodium (purchase this way)
4 green onions (reserve a few for garnish)

reserved egg mixture

...while sauce is thickening…

5. Drain pasta in colander. Rinse under hot water and return to pot. Drizzle olive oil over pasta and toss until slightly coated. Cover to keep warm.

1 tsp olive oil, extra-virgin

...meanwhile…

6. Melt butter in a large nonstick electric or stove-top **fry pan** at med-high.
Add beans, lemon pepper, soy sauce and almonds.
Toss to coat, then **reduce heat** to med-low. Stir often, until beans are hot, glazed, a crunchy, but tender.

Chef-Style Green Beans
1 tsp butter or olive oil
5 cups green or yellow frozen whole beans (1 lb or 450 g) *I like to blend both.*
1/2 tsp lemon pepper
2 tsp soy sauce, reduced-sodium
2 Tbsp matchstick almonds

To serve, ladle hot cream sauce over noodles on individual serving plates. Each person can toss their own! If sauce gets too thick add a little milk to thin it out before serving.

I used to avoid making Carbonara because it ended up being a goopy disaster if I didn't serve it immediately. This version is distraction friendly!

Serves 4-6

DINNER IS READY IN 30 MINUTES

Equipment List:

Large stove-top pot
Large nonstick electric or
   stove-top fry pan
Medium-size stove-top pot
Mixing bowl
Colander
Cutting board
Veggie knife
2 large mixing spoons
Whisk
Pasta fork
Ladle
Measuring cups and spoons

Per serving:

Calories	446
Fat	16.9 g
Protein	20.3 g
Carbohydrate	54.0 g
Fiber	4.0 g
Sodium	369 mg

U.S. Food Exchanges:	Cdn. Food Choices:
3 Starch	3 Carb
2 Meat-lean	3 Meat/Alt
2 Fat	1 1/2 Fat

prep crew
- make sauce
- cook pasta
- saute onion & bacon
- cook green beans

stove-top

20 to prep

The Crunchiest Ever Baked Chicken Fingers with Focaccia and Veggies

Don't change yet! Take out equipment.

Take out ingredients.

1. Preheat **oven** to 500° F.

2. Combine sour cream, mayonnaise and seasoning in a small bowl to make veggie dip. Stir together until smooth. Set aside in **fridge**.

Light Veggie Dip
1/4 cup sour cream, light
1/4 cup mayonnaise, light
1/2 tsp garlic & herb seasoning, salt-free

3. Whisk oil and mayonnaise together in a medium size bowl. Toss chicken filets into bowl and stir to completely coat.

1 1/2 Tbsp canola oil
1 1/2 Tbsp mayonnaise, light
16-20 chicken filets (tenders), boneless, skinless (1 1/2 lbs or 675 g)
or cut chicken breasts into strips

Crumb Coating for Chicken
1 cup corn flake crumbs
(found near coating mixes)
1 tsp original, all purpose seasoning, salt-free
1/2-1 tsp fresh ground pepper *If you like spicy chicken fingers you can use blackened cajun spice instead of pepper.*
waxed paper (or parchment paper)

Combine corn flake crumbs and spice, on a large sheet of wax paper.

Line a cookie sheet with sides, with parchment paper.
Press each piece of chicken into crumbs to completely coat, then arrange on cookie sheet lined with parchment.
Place in **hot oven**. Set timer for 12 minutes.

parchment paper (important)

4. Rinse baby carrots and tomatoes. Rinse cauliflower and break apart into small florets. Rinse and slice cucumber.
Arrange veggies on plate.

2 cups baby carrots
12 cherry or grape tomatoes
1/4 head cauliflower or broccoli
1/2 English cucumber

...when timer rings for chicken...

5. Turn **oven** off then remove chicken.
Place focaccia in oven to warm until chicken is served.
Drizzle oil and vinegar on a plate for dipping the focaccia.

1/2 loaf herbed focaccia
2 Tbsp olive oil, extra-virgin
1 Tbsp balsamic vinegar

Our family likes dipping our chicken fingers in plum sauce, honey or Curry Dip.
The light veggie dip is for your fresh veggies.

plum sauce (optional) *VH is my favorite.*
honey (optional)
Curry Dip (optional) *See page 76.*
Serves 4-6

DINNER IS READY IN 30 MINUTES

Equipment List:
Cookie sheet w/ sides
Medium mixing bowl
Small mixing bowl
Cutting board
Plate
Sharp veggie knife
Bread knife
Whisk
Stirring spoon
Spoon
Measuring cups and spoons
Wax paper
Parchment paper

Per serving:

Calories	493
Fat	17.0 g
Protein	33.6 g
Carbohydrate	52.2 g
Fiber	4.8 g
Sodium	354 mg

U.S. Food Exchanges:	Cdn. Food Choices:
3 Starch	3 1/2 Carb
3 Meat-lean	4 1/2 Meat/Alt
1 1/2 Fat	1 Fat
1 Vegetable	

Prep crew
- make veggie dip
- prep chicken fingers
- rinse veggies
- cut cucumber
- bake chicken fingers
- warm bread
Oven

TAKE 5

15 to prep

4

Honey-Garlic Ribs

I have always liked to boil ribs before BBQing. It gets rid of a bunch of fat and they are fall-off-the-bone tender. Boiling them used to deter me from having ribs in the work week. By letting the slow cooker do the work, ribs aren't just a weekend treat anymore! Teriyaki sauce is a great replacement for honey-garlic sauce. Take-5 - for the veggies.
Vegetarians can still enjoy the benefits of this meal by eating the grilled veggie salad with cashews and soy beans on top.

Mole Chicken

This recipe was as much fun as it was a challenge. I wanted to use easy, family friendly ingredients like chocolate Quik, without compromising an authentic flavor and of course wanted the data healthy. Our families love it!
We made this vegetarian style by sautéing onions, mushrooms, zucchini and adding mixed beans such as black, garbanzo and black-eyed peas. We put this mixture on rice with the sauce over top! Really, really nice!

Southwest Meatloaf

My brother Neil gave me his favorite meat loaf recipe. I made it, but cringed knowing how much fat there was in it! Sooooo as my dear friend Kathy puts it—"I fixed it."
I love the flavor and our test families do too!
Vegetarians can make a sloppy version of this in a pan 'cause you know how hard it is for veggie grind to stay formed... but the sloppy version still has all the flavor!

Chicken & Mushroom Tortellini

Tortellini is often less expensive when you buy it in bulk. It became a mission of mine to find ways to make tortellini dishes that everyone loved. It's one of my favorites. I like things a little spicier, so I always add hot chili flakes to mine.
Vegetarians: Take out the chicken step and it's just as good without.

Lean Sirloin Fajitas

I love the combination of flavors in these fajitas. Our family has no idea they are eating a very healthy meal when we serve this, because it's fun, yet it's loaded with veggies and lean protein. Take 5 - for the veggies.
If you're vegetarian, saute zucchini instead of meat, this is going to be one of your favorite veggie dishes.

On The Menu - Week Five

Honey-Garlic Ribs
with Tossed Grilled Salad

Our Family Rating: 10

Your Family Rating: _____

Mole Chicken
with Rice and Broccoli

Our Family Rating: 10

Your Family Rating: _____

Southwest Meatloaf
with Baby Spuds and Stir-Fry

Our Family Rating: 9

Your Family Rating: _____

Chicken & Mushroom Tortellini
with Veggies & Dip

Our Family Rating: 9.5

Your Family Rating: _____

Lean Sirloin Fajitas
with "The Works"

Our Family Rating: 9.5

Your Family Rating: _____

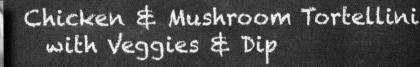

TAKE

Honey-Garlic Ribs with Tossed Grilled Salad

...the night before...
Take out equipment.

Take out ingredients.

1. Cut ribs into slabs and place them upright in crock of **slow cooker** as you cut. Sprinkle onion flakes over top. Add water to completely cover ribs. Cover with lid and set on **low heat** right before you go to bed. (8-9 hours)

   2 1/2 lbs or 1125 g lean pork ribs, back or side (can double the amount to have extras)
   3 Tbsp onion flakes
   water

...in the morning...

2. Transfer ribs to a large cake pan to cool. Once cooled, cover and place in **fridge**.

...when you get home...

3. Preheat **BBQ grill** or **broiler** to medium low-medium (approx **350° F**).
   Spray ribs with cooking spray. Place on BBQ grill or broiler membrane side down. Brush tops with honey-garlic sauce.
   Reduce heat to med-low (**300° F**). Turn ribs often, brushing with remaining sauce.

   cooking spray
   1 jar honey-garlic sauce
   (12 fl oz or 341 mL) *I like VH brand.*
   (or make-your-own honey-garlic sauce by combining 1/4 cup sugar, 1/4 cup honey, 1/2 cup soy sauce, 1 Tbsp molasses, 4 cloves minced garlic, 1/2 cup water)

...meanwhile...

4. Slice peppers, zucchini, onion and mushrooms in large chunks and place in **BBQ grill wok** or pan (or use nonstick fry pan). Dab with pesto.

   1 red bell pepper
   1 green bell pepper
   1 small zucchini
   1 onion
   10 mushrooms
   1 Tbsp basil pesto

   Place on **BBQ grill** (or **stove-top**) at medium. Set timer for 10 minutes, tossing a few times. *You will need to check.*

...meanwhile...

5. Rinse lettuce in basket of salad spinner and spin dry. Arrange on plates.

   1/2 head of Romaine lettuce (3 oz or 90 g)

...when timer rings for veggies...
Remove ribs from **BBQ grill** once you've brushed all the sauce on. Remove veggies from BBQ when tender yet still a little crunchy.
Top salad with grilled veggies. Drizzle with salad dressing.

1/4 cup favorite salad dressing, fat-free

Serve with bread rolls if you like.

6 bread rolls (optional)

<u>**Serves 4-6**</u>

DINNER IS READY IN 30 MINUTES

Equipment List:

...the night before...
Slow cooker
Cutting board
Sharp meat knife & Fork
Large cake pan
...when you get home...
BBQ grill (or broiler pan)
BBQ grill wok
  or nonstick frypan
BBQ tongs
Colander
Cutting board
Salad spinner & Salad tongs
Flipper & Basting brush
Sharp veggie knife
Individual serving plates
Measuring cups and spoons

Per serving:

Calories	475
Fat	28.8 g
Protein	24.6 g
Carbohydrate	29.0 g
Fiber	2.0 g
Sodium	390 mg

U.S. Food Exchanges:	Cdn. Food Choices:
1 1/2 Starch	2 Carb
3 Meat h-fat	3 Meat/Alt
1 Fat	4 Fat
1 Vegetable	

Assumes half honey-garlic
sauce discarded.

prep crew
- cut ribs & cook
  in slow cooker
- remove to cool
- cut veggies
- rinse lettuce
- bbq ribs

BBQ grill/slow cooker

5

20 to prep

Mole Chicken with Rice and Broccoli

Don't change yet! Take out equipment.	**Take out ingredients.**

1. Heat oil in a large nonstick **electric** or **stove-top fry pan** at medium-high. Unroll chicken thighs and place smooth side down, swishing around in the hot oil.

1 tsp olive oil, extra-virgin

10-12 chicken thighs, boneless, skinless (1 3/4 lbs or 800 g)

Sliver onion and add to pan as you cut. Sprinkle with spice and garlic. Turn the chicken over with a fork and brown other side.

1/2 onion
1/2 tsp cinnamon
1/2 tsp coriander
1/2 tsp cumin, ground
2-3 tsp fresh garlic (from a jar)
 (or use cloves)

Soften peanut butter in a medium size bowl in the **microwave** for approx 15-20 seconds. Add salsa, broth and chocolate syrup. Stir to combine. Pour over chicken.

1 Tbsp peanut butter, light
 (or almond butter)
1 cup chunky salsa (mild, medium or hot)
1 cup chicken broth, reduced-sodium
3 Tbsp chocolate syrup (*I use Quik*)

Simmer at medium-low, occasionally spooning sauce over chicken to cover.

2. Combine rice and water in a large microwave safe pot with lid. Place a paper towel under the pot. **Microwave** at high 8 minutes, then medium 8 minutes.

1 1/2 cups basmati or white rice
3 cups water
paper towel

...while rice is cooking...

3. Trim broccoli then rinse in colander or steamer basket. Place water in the bottom of a **stove-top** pot and bring to a full boil with the broccoli in the basket above. Cover and set timer for 3 minutes...
...or microwave at high using a microwave-safe dish with cover for 3 minutes.

1 lb or 450 g broccoli florets (2 heads)
1 cup water

Serve Mole Chicken on hot rice. This is soooo amazing! Toasted sesame seeds on top add a nice flavor and look great!

1 Tbsp sesame seeds, toasted (optional)

Serves 4-6

Equipment List:

Large nonstick electric or
  stove-top fry pan
Large microwave-safe pot
  w/ lid
Stove-top pot w/ steamer
  basket
Colander
Medium size bowl
Cutting board
Sharp veggie knife
Stirring spoon
Fork
Measuring cups and spoons
Paper towel

Per serving:

Calories	421
Fat	9.3 g
Protein	33.9 g
Carbohydrate	50.5 g
Fiber	2.6 g
Sodium	535 mg

U.S. Food Exchanges:	Cdn. Food Choices:
2 1/2 Starch	2 1/2 Carb
4 Meat v-lean	5 Meat/Alt
2 Vegetable	1/2 Other

prep crew
- brown chicken
- sliver onion
- prep sauce
- cook rice
- trim & cook broccoli

stove-top

15 to prep

Southwest Meatloaf with Baby Spuds and Stir-Fry

Don't change yet! Take out equipment.

Take out ingredients.

1. Preheat **oven** to 375º F.
   Combine ground meat, onion flakes, spice, hot pepper relish, eggs, salsa, milk, breadcrumbs and shredded cheese together in a large bowl until well combined. *I use my hands... it's fun!*

   2 lbs or 900 g ground beef, extra-lean (or ground turkey)
   2 Tbsp onion flakes
   1 Tbsp garlic and herb seasoning, salt-free
   2 tsp hot pepper relish (or chopped up jalapeños) (optional)
   2 eggs (or egg whites are even better)
   3/4 cup salsa (mild, medium or hot)
   1/2 cup 1% milk
   1 1/2 cups breadcrumbs
   1/2 cup cheddar cheese, light, shredded

   Form meat onto a **broiler pan** to look like a short, long, wide loaf, no higher than 2" in height. (See page 33 for an illustration of forming a meatloaf.)

   Spread BBQ sauce over top of meatloaf.

   To make your own, combine ketchup, salsa, honey, liquid smoke and Worcestershire sauce in a small bowl. Spread over top of meatloaf.

   1/4 cup southwest BBQ sauce (purchase or make your own)
   <u>**Southwest BBQ Sauce**</u> (optional to make)
   1 cup ketchup
   1/4 cup salsa
   1/4 cup honey
   1 tsp liquid smoke
   2 tsp Worcestershire sauce

   Place meatloaf in preheated **oven**. Set timer for 50 minutes.

2. Wash potatoes and place in medium size oven-safe pan. Toss with olive oil and spice. Place in preheated **oven** beside meatloaf.

   20 red baby potatoes
   1 tsp olive oil, extra-virgin
   1/2 tsp original, all purpose seasoning, salt-free

3. Rinse stir-fry mix in a colander and place in a nonstick **fry pan**. Sprinkle with spice. Let stand.

   4 cups stir-fry mixed vegetables (fresh or frozen) *Oooor... sliver red pepper, slice mushrooms and toss in snap peas.*
   1/2 tsp garlic and herb seasoning, salt-free

   ...when timer rings for meatloaf and potatoes, turn oven off...
   Heat veggies at high. Drizzle with olive oil and toss until heated through.

   1 tsp olive oil, extra-virgin

   ...meanwhile...

4. Sometimes we sprinkle extra cheddar on top of the meatloaf and broil for just a minute until melted. Set a timer for 2 minutes and watch carefully!
   This is a healthier and easier version of my brother Neil's best meatloaf ever.

   1/2 cup cheddar cheese, light, shredded (optional)

   <u>**Serves 6-8**</u>

DINNER IS READY IN 55 MINUTES

Equipment List:

Broiler pan
Medium nonstick fry pan
Medium oven-safe pan
Colander
Large mixing bowl
Cheese grater
2 mixing spoons
Measuring cups and spoons

Per serving:

Calories	489
Fat	16.6 g
Protein	32.3 g
Carbohydrate	52.3 g
Fiber	7.3 g
Sodium	524 mg

U.S. Food Exchanges:	Cdn. Food Choices:
2 1/2 Starch	2 1/2 Carb
4 Meat-lean	4 Meat/Alt
1 Fat	1 Fat
1 Vegetable	1/2 Other

Prep crew
- prep & form meatloaf
- prep potatoes
- rinse & spice veggies
- cook meatloaf,
  potatoes and veggies

Oven/stove-top

20 to prep

Chicken & Mushroom Tortellini with Veggies & Dip

Don't change yet! Take out equipment. **Take out ingredients.**

1. Heat oil in a large **stove-top** pot at medium. Cut chicken into bite size pieces and add to pot as you cut. Season with spice and stir until meat is no longer pink.

1 tsp canola oil
3 chicken breasts, boneless, skinless (1 lb or 450 g)
1 tsp garlic powder
1/2 tsp hot chili flakes (optional)

Dice onion and slice celery adding to pot as you cut.
Rinse and slice mushrooms. Add to pot.

1/2 onion
1 celery rib
5 mushrooms

Add mushroom soup and stir.
Gradually add chicken broth and stir.
Add milk to pot and stir.

1 can mushroom soup, reduced-sodium (10 fl oz or 284 mL)
1 can chicken broth, reduced-sodium (10 fl oz or 284 mL)
2 cups 1% milk

Add tortellini to pot. **Reduce heat** to low to gently boil tortellini. Set timer for 15 minutes or until tortellini is soft. **Stir often.**

4 cups cheese tortellini (12 oz or 350 g) (found in deli or dairy dept) *Tricolor is nice.*

2. Rinse and break off small florets from broccoli and cauliflower. Cut celery into sticks. Arrange with carrots on plate. (or purchase veggies rinseed and cut)

1 lb or 450 g broccoli (2 heads), cauliflower, celery and baby carrots or use precut veggies

Combine mayonnaise, sour cream and spice in a small mixing bowl. Stir and set aside.

Veggie Dip
1/2 cup mayonnaise, light
1/2 cup sour cream, fat-free or light
1/2 tsp garlic & herb seasoning, salt-free

This may look a little watered down while you're making it...but the tortellini ends up puffing up and the sauce ends up being just perfect. You want it a little runny - we serve it in pasta bowls. A little Parmesan on this is delicious!

Parmesan cheese, light, grated (optional)

Serves 4-6

Equipment List:

Large stove-top pot
2 cutting boards
Colander
Small mixing bowl
Serving plate
Sharp meat knife
Sharp veggie knife
Large stirring spoon
Small stirring spoon
Cheese grater
Can opener
Measuring cups and spoons

Per serving:

Calories	493
Fat	15.7 g
Protein	34.3 g
Carbohydrate	53.9 g
Fiber	3.5 g
Sodium	869 mg

U.S. Food Exchanges:	Cdn. Food Choices:
2 1/2 Starch	3 Carb
3 Meat-lean	3 1/2 Meat/Alt
2 Vegetable	1 Fat
1 Fat	1/2 Other
1/2 Milk-low fat	

prep crew
- cut chicken & veggies
- cook chicken & tortellini sauce
- cut veggies
- make dip
stove-top

15 to prep

Lean Sirloin Fajitas with "The Works"

Don't change yet! Take out equipment.

Take out ingredients.

1. Preheat **oven** to 350° F.

2. Heat oil in a large nonstick electric or stove-top **fry pan** or **wok** at med-high. Cut meat into thin strips against the grain and add to pan as you cut.
   Add spices to meat while it's browning. Toss occasionally.

1 tsp canola or olive oil
1 lb or 450 g sirloin steak, lean
We often use boneless flank or chicken breast
1 tsp cumin, ground
1 tsp chili powder
1 tsp fresh garlic (from a jar)
1/4 tsp fresh ground pepper
1/2 tsp hot chili flakes (optional)

Sliver onion and peppers in that order. Add to pan as you cut and stir until onions are brown and slightly soft. **Remove from heat.**

1 small onion (red if possible)
1 small green bell pepper
1 small red bell pepper

Add salsa, Worcestershire sauce and vinegar to meat pan. Stir until well mixed.

3/4 cup chunky salsa (mild, medium or hot)
1 Tbsp Worcestershire sauce
1 Tbsp red wine vinegar

3. When oven is ready, **turn oven off**. Wrap the tortillas up in foil and toss into **prewarmed oven.**

6 flour, multigrain or corn tortillas, 10"
  (choose a lower sodium brand)
aluminum foil

<u>**Toppings**</u>

4. Wash and slice green onion.
   Chop tomatoes and grate cheese.
   Break lettuce into salad spinner, rinse with cold water, and spin dry.

2 green onions
4 Roma tomatoes
1 cup sharp cheddar cheese, grated, light
1/2 head of Romaine lettuce (3 oz or 90 g)

5. Reheat meat mixture when ready to serve.

   Spoon meat and toppings onto center of warmed tortilla. You may enjoy some extra salsa or sour cream in your tortilla.
   Fold up bottom and then fold over sides.

sour cream, fat-free or light (optional)
extra salsa (optional)

<u>**Serves 4-6**</u>

Equipment List:

Large nonstick electric or
  stove-top fry pan or wok
Salad spinner
2 cutting boards
Cheese grater
Sharp meat knife
Sharp veggie knife
Large serving spoon
Large mixing spoon
Measuring cups and spoons
Aluminum foil

Per serving:

Calories	381
Fat	13.5 g
Protein	24.5 g
Carbohydrate	41.2 g
Fiber	3.3 g
Sodium	637 mg

U.S. Food Exchanges:	Cdn. Food Choices:
2 1/2 Starch	2 1/2 Carb
3 Meat-lean	3 1/2 Meat/Alt
1 Vegetable	1 Fat
1 Fat	

prep crew
- brown meat
- cut onion &
  peppers
- prep sauce
- warm tortillas
- cut & prep toppings

stovetop/oven

5

TAKE 5

20 to prep

About The Recipes

Easy Turkey Manicotti

This is one of our test families favorites. When you are stuffing the manicotti, do it with a small spoon over the pan. This isn't a neatness contest, so don't worry if some of the stuff falls out. Only fill them about 3/4 full because the pasta will soften and surround the meat nicely. Once the sauce goes over top, they will come out looking amazing. Note: Don't forget to spray the pan, add the extra liquid, and close the foil very tightly. Take 5 - for the veggie salad.
Vegetarians: Veggie grind is absolutely fantastic in these!

Pesto-Dijon Pork Chops

This is such a wonderful entertaining dish! It always looks great and the pork is always beautiful! The flavor is out of this world!
Vegetarians...poke baker's potatoes with a fork and microwave until the potato can be easily pierced with a knife. Let cool, cut in half and hollow out. Then combine the potato with cheese and broccoli, put the mixture back on top of potato skin with pesto and panko and broil! Really nice! Serve with edamame beans in the shell sautéed with soy sauce and lemon pepper!

Chicken in Crunchy Bread Cups

Remember to butter the bread sparingly before you slice the crusts off, it makes it waaaaay easier. These also freeze beautifully, so they are great thing to make and freeze right after a turkey dinner. Bring these to a potluck and everyone will want the recipe.
Take 5 - for the chicken.
If you are vegetarian you can load these with a blend of mushrooms, use a vegetable broth instead of consommé and use cornstarch to thicken. Remember to up your protein on the salad.

Chinese Meatballs

These meatballs have such a lovely flavor. I'm always asked by people what to do when an Asian or Polynesian dish includes pineapple, but there aren't pineapple fans in the family. Just purchase the large slices, because the juice is usually really important for the flavor. It's often the texture of pineapple in a dish that people don't like. I have to say, I'm a little like that myself. Make up the recipe and then just serve the slices on the side. You'll be amazed how many more people like cold pineapple slices, as opposed to cut up cooked pineapple.

Curried Chicken

If our family doesn't have curried chicken at least once a month they rebel. This is a fantastic pasta sauce and delicious with or without the chicken.

Easy Turkey Manicotti
with Italian Veggies

Our Family Rating: 8.5

Your Family Rating: _____

TAKE 5

Blue

Pesto Dijon Pork Chops
with Roasted Potatoes and Peas

Our Family Rating: 9.5

Your Family Rating: _____

Green

Chicken in Crunchy Bread Cups
with Cranberries and Salad

Our Family Rating: 10

Your Family Rating: _____

TAKE 5

Red

Chinese Meatballs on Rice

Our Family Rating: 8

Your Family Rating: _____

Yellow

Curried Chicken
with Spaghetti and Broccoli

Our Family Rating: 10

Your Family Rating: _____

Red

Easy Turkey Manicotti with Italian Veggies

Don't change yet! Take out equipment.

Take out ingredients.

1. Preheat **oven** to 375° F.
   Brown ground turkey in a large nonstick electric or stove-top **fry pan** or wok at med-high. Add spice and stir. **Remove from heat** when meat is no longer pink.

   Add soup to cooked meat then gradually stir in milk. Mix well to combine.

   Spray lasagna or cake pan with cooking spray. Tip uncooked manicotti on end, in the pan, and spoon filling into shell until it's about 3/4 full. *It doesn't matter if the stuff is falling onto the pan and doesn't look so neat...it looks just beautiful once everything is cooked!*

   When all the shells are filled and side by side in the pan, spoon cottage cheese over top, then spoon pasta sauce over top.

   Sprinkle Parmesan over top and cover tightly with foil. Bake in **preheated oven**. Set timer for 50 minutes.

2. Rinse and chop celery, pepper and cucumber into bite sized chunks. Rinse baby carrots. Place veggies in a medium size bowl.

   Toss with olive oil, balsamic vinegar and spice. Let stand in **fridge**.

   ...when timer rings for manicotti...

3. Remove foil. Grate cheese directly over top. Return the pan to oven and set oven to **broil until cheese starts to bubble**. Set timer for two minutes at a time and watch it very carefully.

Manicotti Filling
1 lb or 450 g ground turkey
1/2 tsp table blend seasoning, salt-free
1 tsp curry powder
1/4 tsp pepper

1 can cream of mushroom soup, reduced-sodium (10 fl oz or 284 mL)
1/4 soup can 1% milk

cooking spray
8 oz or 250 g manicotti noodles

1 cup 1% cottage cheese (8 oz or 250 g)
1 can tomato pasta sauce
  (24 fl oz or 680 mL) *I use a spicy blend.*
  (choose a lower sodium brand)

1/4 cup Parmesan cheese, light, grated
aluminum foil

2 celery ribs
1/2 red bell pepper (or 1 small)
1 cucumber (English or field)
1 cup baby carrots

1 Tbsp olive oil, extra-virgin
1 Tbsp balsamic vinegar
1 tsp Italian seasoning

1 cup grated mozzarella cheese, part-skim, shredded

Serves 4-6

Equipment List:

Large nonstick electric or
   stove-top fry pan or wok
Large lasagna or cake pan
Cutting board
Med-size bowl
Cheese grater
Can opener
Sharp veggie knife
2 large serving spoons
Large stirring spoon
Measuring cups and spoons
Aluminum foil

Per serving:

Calories	483
Fat	15.4 g
Protein	32.2 g
Carbohydrate	52.0 g
Fiber	5.4 g
Sodium	959 mg

U.S. Food Exchanges:	Cdn. Food Choices:
2 Starch	3 Carb
3 1/2 Meat-lean	4 1/2 Meat/Alt
2 Vegetable	1/2 Fat
1 Fat	
1/2 Milk-fat free	

prep crew
- brown meat
- prep filling
- assemble
- cut veggies
& toss in
vinaigrette
stove-top/oven

TAKE 5

20 to prep

6

Pesto-Dijon Pork Chops with Roasted Potatoes and Peas

Don't change yet! Take out equipment.

Take out ingredients.

1. Preheat **oven** to 450° F.

2. Place potatoes in a metal lasagna or cake pan. If the baby potatoes are large, cut them in half. Drizzle with olive oil and sprinkle with spice. Toss to completely coat, then place in **oven** (even if oven is not fnished preheating).

20 baby potatoes (or 4 large, thin skin, cut into smaller chunks)
1 tsp olive oil, extra-virgin
1/2 tsp original, all purpose seasoning, salt-free

3. Rinse peas in colander or steamer basket. Place water in the bottom of a stove-top pot. Let stand with **no heat**.

3 cups frozen baby peas
1 cup water

4. Combine pesto and Dijon in a small bowl or cup.
Place pork chops on an oven-safe metal pan. Spread pesto-Dijon mixture evenly over each pork chop. Sprinkle with panko flakes.

1/4 cup basil pesto (found near pasta sauces)
1 Tbsp Dijon mustard
4 large pork loin chops, 1/2" thick, boneless, trimmed (1 1/2 lbs or 675 g) (thickness of chop is important or they will be overcooked)
1/4 cup panko flakes or cornflake crumbs (found near coating mixes) *Bug your local grocery store to carry these if they don't have them. These are great to have on hand!*

Once temperature reaches 450° F, **reduce heat** to 425° F. Place pork chops in **oven** beside potatoes. Set timer for 20 minutes.

...when timer rings...
5. Bring water to a full boil with the peas in the basket above. Cover and set timer for 3 minutes...
...or microwave at high for 3-4 minutes using a microwave-safe dish with cover. Let stand.

...meanwhile...
6. Remove potatoes from oven when pierced easily with a knife.

7. **Broil** pork chops until tops are just brown. Set timer for 2-3 minutes and watch carefully! *You don't want a burnt mess!*

Expect the pesto-Dijon on the chops to be moist. The panko only adds a tiny bit of crunch. Texture-flavor is yum!

Serves 4-6

Equipment List:

Oven-safe metal pan
Metal lasagna or cake pan
Stove-top pot w/ steamer
  basket
Colander
Small bowl or cup
Sharp veggie knife
Stirring spoon
Measuring cups and spoons

Per serving:

Calories	381
Fat	8.7 g
Protein	34.5 g
Carbohydrate	40.9 g
Fiber	6.7 g
Sodium	405 mg

U.S. Food Exchanges:	Cdn. Food Choices:
2 Starch	2 1/2 Carb
4 1/2 Meat-lean	5 Meat/Alt
1 Vegetable	

prep crew
- assemble
- no cutting or chopping
- cook potatoes, chops & veggies

stovetop/oven

15 to prep

6

Chicken in Crunchy Bread Cups with Cranberries and Salad

Don't change yet! Take out equipment.

Take out ingredients.

1. Preheat **oven** to 400° F.

   Combine cornstarch, gravy mix, consommé and spice in a **stove-top** pot at no heat. Turn heat to medium and whisk constantly until thickened. **Remove from heat**.

   Finely dice chicken and add to pot as you cut. Finely chop green onions and mushrooms adding to pot as you cut. Stir to combine. Set aside.

2. Butter each slice of bread sparingly, then slice off crusts and discard.
   Press bread slices, butter side down, into muffin tins.

3. Spoon chicken mixture evenly over bread in muffin cups.

   Place in preheated **oven** on lower rack. Set timer for 15 minutes or until golden.

   …meanwhile…
4. Rinse lettuce leaves in salad spinner and spin dry. Transfer spinach to serving plates. Sliver red pepper. Sprinkle over spinach. Top with cashews if you wish. Drizzle with salad dressing.

   …when timer rings for chicken cups...
   Spoon cranberry sauce over hot chicken cups or have them plain. Serve alongside salad.

   If you double this recipe leftovers freeze beautifully and are great for entertaining or a quick grab-and-go lunch.

<u>Chicken Mixture</u>
1 Tbsp cornstarch
1 Tbsp dry brown gravy mix *I like Bisto.*
1 can consommé soup (10 fl oz or 284 mL)
1/2 tsp curry powder
1/2 tsp poultry seasoning
1/2 of one cooked deli roaster chicken
  (3 cups cooked diced chicken)
2 green onions
5 small mushrooms

2 1/4 tsp butter, softened (for all)
1 loaf bread, multigrain, sliced (18 slices)

reserved chicken mixture

You may need to cook them a little longer, depending on your oven.

1 bag spinach (6 oz or 170 g)

1/2 red pepper
1/4 cup cashews, unsalted (optional)
1/4 cup salad dressing, light, fruit vinaigrette or your favorite
  (choose a lower sodium brand)

1/2 cup whole berry cranberry sauce

<u>Serves 4</u>
Makes 18 chicken cups.
Assumes 6 leftover.

DINNER IS READY IN 30 MINUTES

Equipment List:

Stove-top pot
Small muffin tins
2 cutting boards
Salad spinner
Salad tongs
Sharp meat knife
Sharp veggie knife
Stirring spoon
Whisk
Can opener
Butter knife
Mixing spoon
Measuring cups and spoons
Individual serving plates

Per serving:

Calories	396
Fat	10.0 g
Protein	28.5 g
Carbohydrate	48.9 g
Fiber	6.2 g
Sodium	785 mg

U.S. Food Exchanges:	Cdn. Food Choices:
3 Starch	3 Carb
3 Meat-lean	3 Meat/Alt

Assumes six chicken cups leftover.

prep crew
- cut chicken & veggies
- prep mixture
- butter bread
- cut off crusts
- assemble
- cut & prep salad

stove-top/oven

TAKE 5

15
to
prep

6

Chinese Meatballs on Rice

Don't change yet! Take out equipment.

Take out ingredients.

1. Combine rice and water in a large microwave-safe pot with lid. Place a paper towel under the pot. **Microwave** at high 8 minutes.

1 1/4 cups basmati or white rice
2 1/2 cups water
paper towel

    ...meanwhile...

2. Form ground beef into 1" size meatballs. (Place in fry pan as you form, unless forming meatballs ahead of time.)
    Add to a large nonstick electric or stove-top **fry pan** at medium heat. Flip meatballs over to brown other side.
    Rinse and chop pepper into small chunks, adding to pan as you cut.
    Add garlic and spices to pan and stir.

1 1/2 lbs or 675 g ground beef, extra-lean

1 green bell pepper
  (or use 1/2 red and 1/2 green)
2 tsp prepared garlic (from a jar)
1/2 tsp table blend seasoning, salt-free
1/4 tsp fresh ground pepper

    Measure cornstarch into a 2 cup measuring cup or bowl. Very gradually whisk pineapple juice, from the can of pineapple, into the cornstarch using a whisk or fork. (Set aside pineapple chunks.) Add vinegar to juice.
    Pour juice over fully cooked meatballs.

2 Tbsp cornstarch
1 cup pineapple juice
  (juice from a can of unsweetened pineapple chunks, 20 fl oz or 540 mL can size)
2 Tbsp vinegar

    In the unrinsed measuring cup combine sugar, beef broth and soy sauce.
    Pour mixture into pan.

1/2 cup brown sugar
1 cup beef broth, reduced-sodium
  (or use chicken broth)
1 Tbsp soy sauce, reduced-sodium

    Add pineapple chunks to pan (a little or a lot, depending on your preference.) Set remainder of pineapple aside.
    Reduce heat to a high simmer.

1 cup of reserved pineapple chunks
  (leave out if you're not a pineapple fan)

    **...when done prepping meatballs
     and sauce...**

3. Add peas and pea pods to rice. *Careful it's hot!* Stir and return rice to microwave for 8 minutes at medium heat. Rest rice 5 minutes.

10 oz or 300 g frozen pea pods
1 cup frozen baby peas

    Serve the meatballs and sauce on the rice or on the side.

<u>**Serves 4-6**</u>

DINNER IS READY IN 30 MINUTES

Equipment List:

Large nonstick electric or
  stove-top fry pan
Large microwave-safe pot
  w/ lid
Cutting board
2 cup measuring cup or
  bowl
Can opener
Flipper
Whisk or fork
Sharp veggie knife
2 large stirring spoons
Measuring cups and spoons
Paper towel

Per serving:

Calories	499
Fat	12.6 g
Protein	27.0 g
Carbohydrate	68.8 g
Fiber	4.3 g
Sodium	291 mg

U.S. Food Exchanges:	Cdn. Food Choices:
2 1/2 Starch	3 1/2 Carb
3 Meat-lean	3 Meat/Alt
2 Vegetable	1 Fat
1 Fruit	1 Other
1 Fat	

Prep crew
- cook rice
- cut green pepper
- prep meatballs
- cook meatballs
  in sauce
- add peas to rice

stove-top/
microwave

20
to
prep

Curried Chicken with Spaghetti and Broccoli

Don't change yet! Take out equipment.   **Take out ingredients.**

1. Heat oil in a large nonstick electric or stove-top **fry pan** or wok at medium heat.

   Cut chicken into bite size pieces and gradually add to pan as you cut. Toss until the meat is no longer pink. Add garlic and spices to pan while meat is browning. Stir.

   Chop onion adding to chicken as you cut. Rinse and slice mushrooms adding to pan as you cut. If you like green pepper then rinse, chop and add to pan.

2. Fill a large **stove-top pot** with water and bring to a boil for pasta.

3. Add soup to chicken mixture and gradually stir in milk. Continue to stir until well blended.
   Simmer at medium heat, stirring often until pasta is ready.

4. Place pasta in boiling water, stir and cook uncovered. Set timer for 9 minutes or follow package directions.

5. Trim broccoli then rinse in colander or steamer basket. Place water in the bottom of a stove-top pot and bring to a full boil with the broccoli in the basket above. Cover and set timer for 3 minutes...
   ...or microwave at high using a microwave-safe dish with cover for 3 minutes. Let stand.

   ..when timer rings for pasta...
6. Rinse pasta under hot water in a colander. Return to pot and cover, **no heat**. Toss with basil and drizzle with olive oil if you like.

   Serve chicken over pasta or on the side and sprinkle with Parmesan.

Ingredients:

1 tsp olive oil or canola oil

Chicken Mixture
3 chicken breasts, boneless, skinless (1 lb or 450 g)
2 tsp garlic (from a jar)
2 tsp basil, dried
4 tsp curry powder
1/8 tsp cayenne pepper

1 small onion
12 mushrooms
1/2 green bell pepper

water

1 can cream of mushroom soup, reduced-sodium (10 fl oz or 284 mL)
1/2 the soup can 1% milk

12 oz or 340 g spaghetti pasta

1 lb or 450 g broccoli florets (2 heads)

1/2 tsp basil, dried
1 tsp olive oil, extra virgin (optional)

2 Tbsp Parmesan cheese, light, grated (optional)
Serves 4-6

Equipment List:

Large nonstick electric or
   stove-top fry pan or wok
Large stove-top pot
Stove-top pot w/
   steamer basket
Colander
2 cutting boards
Sharp meat knife
Sharp veggie knife
Can opener
Pasta fork
Stirring spoon
Measuring cups and spoons

prep crew

- cut & brown chicken
- rinse & cut veggies
- cook sauce, pasta
  & veggies

stove-top

15
to
prep

Spinach & Cheese Stuffed Pasta

These little puppies are addictive. They are easy to make and they are a great entertaining dish. I like to do the first four steps the night before. It only takes a few minutes and it makes the dinner even easier than it already is. If you like to entertain, I suggest you make double and freeze them individually on a sprayed cookie sheet. Once frozen, toss them in a freezer bag. Bake them fresh with the sauce, just before the guests arrive.

Take 5 - for the pasta.

Roasted Apricot & Pesto Chicken

This is amazing! It's ok to leave the skin on the chicken sometimes! When you are Eating Forward™ and know what you are having for dinner that night, you simply adjust your fat intake in the day and ENJOY! This combo is really nice.

Tangy Meatballs

This is just delicious, one of my favorite meatball recipes. Make sure you don't boil down the sauce too much, because it's wonderful on the rice.

Take 5 - for the veggie...whether you are Cooking Together/Apart or not. It will turn this recipe from quick to super quick.

Ginger Beef & Snap Peas

This doesn't taste like your average one-pan meal. Aaand if you're wondering why I always put optional beside cilantro (also known as fresh coriander or Chinese parsley) it's because cilantro is just one of those things you either love or hate. Ron and I used to hate it but we're both addicted to it now!

Vegetarians, veggie grind is great in this dish!

Spicy Crispy Chicken Burgers

Over the top! This is my all time favorite chicken burger! I'm telling you though...gorgonzola or cambozola cheese with the hot pepper jelly takes this to the next level! The crunchy with the creamy with the little bite...ooooooohh, ok, I'm salivating!

Vegetarians, the coated veggie chicken works really well!

On The Menu - Week Seven

Spinach & Cheese Stuffed Pasta Shells with Caesar Salad

Our Family Rating: 9

Your Family Rating: _____

TAKE 5

Roasted Apricot & Pesto Chicken with Baby Potatoes & Asparagus

Our Family Rating: 10

Your Family Rating: _____

Tangy Meatballs with Rice and Italian Tossed Veggies

Our Family Rating: 8.5

Your Family Rating: _____

TAKE 5

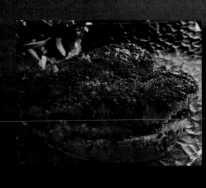

Ginger Beef & Snap Peas with Egg Noodles

Our Family Rating: 10

Your Family Rating: _____

Spicy Crispy Chicken Burgers with Dipping Veggies

Our Family Rating: 10

Your Family Rating: _____

Blue

Green

Red

Yellow

Yellow

Spinach & Cheese Stuffed Pasta Shells with Caesar Salad

Don't change yet! Take out equipment.

Take out ingredients.

1. Preheat **oven** to **375° F**.

2. Fill a large **stove-top** pot with water and bring to a boil for pasta.
   ...meanwhile...

   water

3. Drain spinach in a colander, using a fork to lightly squeeze out some of the water from the spinach.
   Combine drained spinach, egg and cheeses together in a medium size mixing bowl.
   Finely chop or shred shallot. Add to bowl.
   Add oil and stir. Cover and set aside in **fridge**.

   <u>Spinach and Cheese Stuffing</u>
   3 1/2 oz or 100 g frozen chopped spinach, defrosted *You can run water over spinach in a colander to defrost quickly.*
   1 egg
   1/3 cup feta cheese, light, crumbled
   1 cup ricotta cheese
   1/4 cup Parmesan cheese, light, grated
   1/2 cup mozzarella cheese, part-skim, shredded
   1/2 cup cottage cheese, 1%
   1 shallot
   1 tsp olive oil, extra-virgin
   1 large freezer bag

4. Add pasta to boiling water and **reduce heat** to a medium boil. Set timer for 5 minutes. (You just want them softened, not completely cooked.)
   ...when timer rings for pasta...
   Drain pasta in a colander then rinse under cold water.
   Return to pot and gently toss with olive oil.

   24 large pasta shells (conchiglioni rigati) 8 oz or 225 g

   1/2 tsp olive oil, extra-virgin

5. Stuff spinach mixture into each shell with a small spoon and place, stuffed side up, in a large lasagna or cake pan.
   Cover with pasta sauce.
   Place in preheated **oven**. Set timer for 30 minutes.
   ...when timer rings for stuffed pasta...
   Remove pasta from **oven** and let stand.

   reserved spinach mixture
   reserved pasta shells

   1 can tomato-basil pasta sauce (24 fl oz or 680 mL) *I use the spicy variety.* (choose a lower sodium brand.)

6. Rinse lettuce in basket of salad spinner and spin dry. Place in large bowl and add bacon bits, croutons and Parmesan cheese if you wish. Toss with salad dressing.

   1 bag Romaine lettuce (6 oz or 170 g)
   bacon bits, croutons and Parmesan cheese (optional)
   1/3 cup of Caesar salad dressing, light

   <u>Serves 4-6</u>

114   DINNER IS READY IN 50 MINUTES

Equipment List:

Large lasagna or cake pan
Large stove-top pot
Cutting board
Colander
Medium mixing bowl
Salad spinner
Salad bowl
Salad tongs
Can opener
2 stirring spoons
Fork
Small spoon
Sharp veggie knife
Measuring cups and spoons
Large freezer bag

Per serving:

Calories	394
Fat	13.1 g
Protein	21.1 g
Carbohydrate	46.9 g
Fiber	4.9 g
Sodium	789 mg

U.S. Food Exchanges:	Cdn. Food Choices:
3 Starch	3 Carb
2 Meat-lean	3 Meat/Alt
1 Fat	1 Fat

Prep crew
- part cook pasta shells
- cut shallot
- prep stuffing & shells
- prep salad
- bake pasta

stove-top/oven

TAKE 5

20 to prep

Roasted Apricot & Pesto Chicken with Baby Potatoes and Asparagus

Don't change yet! Take out equipment.

Take out ingredients.

1. Preheat **oven** to 450° F.

2. Wash potatoes and place in a small oven-safe pan on middle rack. Drizzle with olive oil and sprinkle with spice. Toss potatoes until well coated. Place in **oven** (don't wait for oven to preheat).

20 baby potatoes (2 lbs or 900 g)
  (or 4 large, cut into chunks)
  (if baby potatoes are large, cut in half)
1 tsp olive oil, extra-virgin
1/2 tsp original, all purpose seasoning, salt-free

   ...meanwhile...

3. Combine jam and pesto in a small mixing bowl and stir until well combined.

1 Tbsp apricot jam (or fig or peach jam)
2 Tbsp basil pesto

   Lift skin of each chicken breast and spread 1/4 of the mixture under the middle of each skin. Sprinkle tops of chicken breast with pepper. **Reduce heat** to 400° F.
   Place chicken in a different oven-safe pan.
   Place in **oven** beside potatoes.
   You can use one large pan for both, but the potatoes get greasy.
   Set timer for 35 minutes or until internal temperature is 170° F in the thickest part of chicken.

4 chicken breasts with skin, bone in
  (1 3/4 lb or 800 g)
1/2 tsp fresh ground pepper for all

Use an instant read thermometer to ensure the chicken is cooked through. They are only a few bucks and really help you to know when dinner is ready.

4. Snap off bottom nodes of asparagus and discard. *See page 35.* Rinse in colander or steamer basket. Place water in the bottom of a **stove-top** pot. Let stand **no heat**.

20 asparagus spears (1 lb or 450 g)

1 cup water

   ...just before chicken and potatoes are ready...
   Bring water to a full boil with the asparagus in the basket above. Cover and set timer for 4 minutes...
   ...or microwave in a microwave-safe dish wth cover for the 4 minutes.
   Drain water and toss in pot with butter if you like.

butter (optional)

   ...when timer rings...
   Remove chicken and potatoes from oven.

<u>Serves 4-6</u>

If you want to make the chicken ahead for company, it freezes beautifully raw.

DINNER IS READY IN 55 MINUTES

Equipment List:

2 oven-safe pans
Stove-top pot w/ steamer
  basket
Colander
Small mixing bowl
Cutting board
Stirring spoon
Sharp veggie knife
Instant read thermometer
Measuring cups and spoons

Per serving:

Calories	368
Fat	13.9 g
Protein	29.3 g
Carbohydrate	32.1 g
Fiber	5.1 g
Sodium	118 mg

U.S. Food Exchanges:	Cdn. Food Choices:
2 Starch	2 Carb
3 1/2 Meat-lean	4 Meat/Alt
1 Fat	1/2 Fat

1/4 lb of chicken is bone and excess skin.

prep crew

- prep & cook chicken, potatoes & asparagus
- no cutting or chopping

stove-top/oven

15 to prep

Tangy Meatballs with Rice and Italian Tossed Veggies

Don't change yet! Take out equipment.

Take out ingredients.

1. Bring water to a boil in a large **stove-top** pot at high. Use a lid when boiling, it speeds up the process.

water

   Form ground beef into 1" size meatballs. Drop meatballs into boiling water. Toss occasionally to ensure all have been submerged. After the last meatball has been added to the water and the water has reached a full boil, set timer for 5 minutes.

1 1/2 lb or 675 g extra-lean ground beef

   Dice and add onion to another large **stove-top** pot. Add the following to onion pot; tomato paste, brown sugar, vinegar, water, spices and Worcestershire sauce. Let stand, **no heat**.

<u>Tangy Meatball Sauce</u>
1 small onion or 2 Tbsp onion flakes
1 can tomato paste (5 1/2 fl oz or 156 mL)
  (choose a lower sodium brand)
1/2 cup brown sugar
1/2 cup vinegar
1 1/3 cup water
1 1/2 tsp paprika
1/8 tsp celery salt
2 Tbsp Worcestershire sauce

   ...meanwhile...
2. Combine rice and water in a large microwave-safe pot with lid. Place a paper towel under the pot. **Microwave** at high 8 minutes, then medium 8 minutes.

1 1/2 cups basmati or white rice
3 cups water
paper towel
Note: *When using a microwave for rice, water may spill over depending on the pot you're using. The paper towel makes for easy clean-up. Let the rice stand for about 5 minutes after cooking... about the time it takes to set the table.*

   ...when timer rings for meatballs...
3. Transfer meatballs using a slotted spoon into the tangy meatball sauce pot. Heat on **stove-top** at medium-low for 10-15 minutes or until rice is ready. *Stir occasionally to get that nummy sauce all over them!!!*

4. Rinse carrots and snap peas. Place in a salad bowl. Rinse cauliflower and break off small florets with your fingers adding to bowl as you break.
   Rinse and sliver red pepper and add to bowl. Drizzle with dressing and toss to coat.

1 cup baby carrots
1 cup snap peas
1/4 head cauliflower

1/2 red bell pepper
2 Tbsp Italian dressing, light
  (or use precut veggies from produce dept)

When removing the rice, careful it's hot!

<u>Serves 4-6</u>

DINNER IS READY IN 30 MINUTES

Equipment List:

2 Large stove-top pots
  w/ lids
Large microwave-safe pot
  w/ lid
Colander
Salad bowl
Cutting board
Sharp veggie knife
Stirring spoon
Large slotted spoon
Measuring cups and spoons
Paper Towel

Per serving:

Calories	491
Fat	12.7 g
Protein	26.4 g
Carbohydrate	68.9 g
Fiber	5.2 g
Sodium	440 mg

U.S. Food Exchanges:	Cdn. Food Choices:
3 Starch	3 Carb
3 1/2 Meat-lean	4 Meat/Alt
1 1/2 Other	1 1/2 Other

1/4 lb of chicken is bone and excess skin.

prep crew
- form & cook meatballs
- cut onion
- prep sauce
- cook rice
- rinse & cut veggies

stove-top/
microwave

TAKE 5

15
to
prep

Ginger Beef with Egg Noodles and Snap Peas

Don't change yet! Take out equipment.	**Take out ingredients.**

1. Fill a large **stove-top** pot with water and bring to a boil for noodles.

water

2. Heat oil in a large nonstick electric or stove-top **fry pan** or wok at low heat. Finely chop green onions, adding to pan as you cut (Set aside 1/4 cup green onions for garnish). Sauté for 2-3 minutes. Add garlic and ginger to pan.

1 tsp canola oil
1 bunch green onions (1 cup chopped)

2 Tbsp fresh garlic (from a jar)
  (or 2 Tbsp freshly minced)
1 Tbsp fresh ginger (from a jar)
  (or 1 Tbsp fresh grated)

Increase heat to medium high. Add beef to fry pan. Break up the beef with a spoon. Brown until no longer pink.

1 lb or 450 g extra-lean ground beef
  (or use pork)

Rinse snap peas in a colander and to pan. Slice zucchini into long wedges, adding to pan as you cut.

1 cup snap peas
1/2 of a small zucchini

Add soy sauce, chili sauce, vinegar, sesame oil, chili flakes, water and cilantro to pan and stir. (If using cilantro rinse a little extra for those who love it as a garnish.)

1/4 cup soy sauce, reduced-sodium
1/4 cup sweet chili sauce
2 Tbsp rice vinegar
1 Tbsp sesame oil
1/4 - 1 tsp hot chili flakes
1 cup water
2 Tbsp cilantro (optional)

3. Drop noodles into boiling water. Set timer for 6 minutes. When timer rings, drain into large colander then toss into meat pan. Stir to completely coat noodles in sauce making sure all ingredients are well combined.
Reduce heat to medium. Set timer for 3 minutes. Stir again right before serving.

3/4 lb or 340 g broad egg noodles
I like No Yolks brand.

4. Rinse extra snap peas and serve on the side.

2 cups snap peas

Sprinkle individual plates of Ginger Beef, if you'd like, with the extra sliced green onion and cilantro.

green onion (optional)
cilantro (optional)

Serves 4-6

DINNER IS READY IN 30 MINUTES

Equipment List:

Large stove-top pot
Large nonstick electric or
   stove-top fry pan or wok
Large nonstick fry pan
   or wok
Medium serving bowl
2 small serving bowls
Cutting board
Colander
Sharp veggie knife
Mixing spoon
Measuring cups and spoons

Per serving:

Calories	397
Fat	9.4 g
Protein	25.1 g
Carbohydrate	53.8 g
Fiber	3.4 g
Sodium	532 mg

U.S. Food Exchanges:	Cdn. Food Choices:
3 Starch	3 1/2 Carb
2 Meat-lean	2 Meat/Alt
1 Vegetable	
1/2 Fat	

prep crew
- cut green onion
  & zucchini
- brown meat
- cook noodles
- rinse snap peas
- assemble

stove-top

20 to prep

Spicy Crispy Chicken Burgers with Dipping Veggies

Don't change yet! Take out equipment.

Take out ingredients.

1. Preheat **oven** to 450° F.

2. Slice tomatoes and sliver onion for burger toppings. Rinse lettuce leaves, cover and set aside in **fridge**.

   Rinse cucumber, snap peas, celery, tomatoes and carrots. Cut celery into sticks and slice cucumber. Arrange veggies on a serving plate. (People can even munch on this part while you're making the burgers.)

   Burger Toppings
   2 tomatoes
   1/4 red onion
   2 cups lettuce leaves

   1 English cucumber
   1 cup snap peas
   2 celery ribs
   8-12 cherry tomatoes
   2 cups baby carrots
   Caesar or ranch dressing, light, for dip
   (optional)

3. Place cornflake crumbs on a sheet of waxed paper. *If your family likes spicy food, you can also add cayenne or chipotle pepper.*

   Place parchment paper on a cookie sheet with sides. Whisk oil and mayonnaise together in a small bowl. Smear an even amount over both sides of a piece of chicken. (*You can use the back of a spoon, but I like to use my hands.*) Press chicken onto crumbs. Flip and press until completely coated and transfer to parchment paper.
   Repeat for each piece of chicken. Wash hands when done! Place chicken pan into preheated **oven**. Set timer for 15 minutes.

   1 cup cornflake crumbs
   (or panko flakes, found near coating mixes)
   waxed paper
   1/4 tsp cayenne or chipotle pepper
   (optional)
   parchment paper (very important)
   1 Tbsp canola or olive oil
   2 Tbsp mayonnaise, light
   4 chicken cutlets (1 1/3 lbs or 600 g)
   (or butterflied chicken breasts as shown)
   See page 33 for how to butterfly chicken
   Note: the cooked chicken is huge so most people will only want half a chicken breast in their bun!

   ...meanwhile...

4. Spread cambozola cheese on one side of the bun and red pepper jelly on the other.

   ...when timer rings for chicken...
   Turn oven off. Chicken is ready if internal temperature is 170° F. Take chicken out and put buns in. Set timer for 2 minutes.

   Sandwich this delicious crispy burger inside this yummy warm bun...That's it...I need to have this for dinner tonight!

   6 hamburger buns, multigrain
   1 1/2 Tbsp cambozola cheese for all
   (or cream cheese)
   2 Tbsp red pepper jelly for all (found near gourmet condiments) or use apple jelly

   Use an instant read thermometer to ensure the chicken is cooked through. They are only a few bucks and really help you to know when dinner is ready.

   <u>Serves 4-6</u>

DINNER IS READY IN 30 MINUTES

Equipment List:

Cookie sheet w/ sides
Baking pan
Small mixing bowl
Cutting board
Colander
Sharp veggie knife
Sharp bread knife
Serving plate
Whisk
Butter knife
Instant read thermometer
Measuring cups and spoons
Waxed paper
Parchment paper

Per serving:

Calories	450
Fat	10.4 g
Protein	33.3 g
Carbohydrate	58.3 g
Fiber	5.9 g
Sodium	606 mg

U.S. Food Exchanges:	Cdn. Food Choices:
3 Starch	3 1/2 Carb
4 Meat-lean	4 1/2 Meat/Alt
1 Vegetable	

2 Tbsp panko flakes are left over.

prep crew
- cut veggies & toppings
- prep burgers
- bake burgers

Oven

20 to prep

About The Recipes

Sloppy Beef on a Bun

This is the fun-food meal of the week. I have to admit, I really feel like a kid again when we have this. When you mix a little fresh fruit in with the fruit cocktail, it gives a fresh fruit flavor with way less cutting and chopping. In the summer, I may use all fresh fruit with this. If I'm in a real rush, I may only use the fruit cocktail. Look at your timeline and adjust accordingly. Vegetarians can replace the beef with veggie grind and it works just fine.

Chili-Glazed Chicken

Yum, yum, yum! There is nothing left to say other than that! Okay, just one thing—one test family found this dry even though they loved the flavor. I recommend you set the timer for less time the first time you make it, then check its doneness, juuuust in case your oven's temp is off and cooks hot! This is one of my favorite thigh recipes!

Spinach & Cheese Ravioli

This meal is easy and delicious! Our test families pointed out two things. The first is to make all the sauce. The proportion of sauce to pasta is great. The other thing is that you really need to wait until you're ready to eat before folding the sauce into the pasta, so it doesn't dry out.

Savory Pot Roast

Night Before recipe - Nummy, nummy!!! This is such a great "night before preparation" because there is almost nothing to do and you can stick the frozen solid roast into the slow cooker. I call this my life saver meal. I always feel like I've served my family a home cooked meal...and I've done almost nothing!!!

Teriyaki Chicken Toss

This is a family hit and fantastic meat free. I love adding the broth and curry to the noodles and most of our test families love it too. If you're not a curry fan just leave it out and it's still amazing... but try it first... you might be surprised.
Take 5 - for the veggies.

124

Sloppy Beef on a Bun
with Mixed Fruit

Our Family Rating: 9

Your Family Rating: _____

Chili-Glazed Chicken
with Rice and Broccoli

Our Family Rating: 9.5

Your Family Rating: _____

Spinach & Cheese Ravioli in a
Maple-Tomato Sauce w/
Green Beans

Our Family Rating: 9

Your Family Rating: _____

Savory Pot Roast
with Harvest Vegetables

Our Family Rating: 10

Your Family Rating: _____

Teriyaki Chicken Toss
with Spaghettini Pasta

Our Family Rating: 10

Your Family Rating: _____

TAKE

Sloppy Beef on a Bun with Mixed Fruit

Don't change yet! Take out equipment.   **Take out ingredients.**

1. Preheat **oven** to 375º F.

2. Brown meat in a large nonstick electric or stove-top **fry pan** at med-high until meat is no longer pink.
   Add ketchup, salsa, water, onion flakes, prepared mustard and Worcestershire sauce to fully cooked meat.

   Stir, then **reduce heat** to a low simmer.

1 1/2 lbs or 675 g ground beef, extra-lean

1/2 cup ketchup
1/2 cup salsa (or replace salsa with ketchup)
1/2 cup water
1 Tbsp onion flakes
1 Tbsp prepared mustard
1 Tbsp Worcestershire sauce

3. Slice buns and place them open side up on oven rack in preheated **oven**.
   Now, **turn oven off!**
   Crazy you say? No way, this is the most amazing way to warm buns in the oven.

4-6 hamburger buns, whole wheat
Serve open faced or as a sloppy hamburger.

   ...meanwhile...
4. Wash grapes and pull apart mandarins. Mix together with fruit cocktail in a medium bowl.
   It looks great if you serve it in a short glass of some kind.
   Garnish fruit with a spoonful of vanilla yogurt.

1 1/2 cups red grapes
3 mandarins
1 can fruit salad, unsweetened
 (14 fl oz or 398 mL) (1 3/4 cups)
 1/2 cup vanilla yogurt, low-fat

   When ready to sit down and eat, spoon meat sauce onto warm bun (serve half a bun at a time) and sprinkle cheese on top. *Yuuuumy!!!* If meat mixture is too saucy simmer for a few minutes longer. You may need a knife and fork.

1/2 cup cheddar cheese, light, shredded

Serves 4-6

Equipment List:

Large nonstick electric or
  stove-top fry pan
Medium bowl
Cutting board
Bread knife
Cheese grater
Can opener
Stirring spoon
Spoon
Measuring cups and spoons

Per serving:

Calories	428
Fat	15.5 g
Protein	28.3 g
Carbohydrate	46.7 g
Fiber	4.6 g
Sodium	679 mg

U.S. Food Exchanges:	Cdn. Food Choices:
2 Starch	3 Carb
3 Meat	4 Meat/Alt
1 Fat	1 Fat
1 Fruit	

prep crew

- cook meat & sauce
- wash & prep fruit salad
- grate cheese

stove-top/oven

20 to prep

8

Chili-Glazed Chicken with Rice and Broccoli

Don't change yet! Take out equipment.

Take out ingredients.

1. Preheat **oven** to 350° F.

2. Combine rice and water in a large oven-safe pot. Stir. Cover and place in **oven.** (oven doesn't have to be fully preheated)

   1 1/2 cups basmati or white rice (or mixed rice - *I like Canoe brand*)
   3 cups of water

3. Stir cumin, chili powder, balsamic vinegar, honey and chicken broth together in the bottom of a 9"x13" oven-safe baking dish or pan using a fork.

   1/2 tsp cumin, ground
   1 tsp chili powder
   2 Tbsp balsamic vinegar
   2 Tbsp honey (liquid or softened)
   1/4 cup chicken broth, reduced-sodium

   Unroll thighs and place flat on top of combined ingredients in pan. *Squish them together if you need to.* Spoon all the sauce evenly over chicken pieces. Place in preheated **oven** beside rice. Set timer for 40 minutes or until internal temperature is 170° F.

   10-12 chicken thighs, boneless, skinless or 4-6 chicken breasts **(1 3/4 lbs or 800 g)**

   Use an instant read thermometer to ensure the chicken is cooked through, They are only a few bucks and really help you to know when dinner is ready.

4. Trim broccoli then rinse in colander or steamer basket. Place water in the bottom of a **stovetop** pot with broccoli in the basket above. Let stand with **no heat**.

   1 lb or 450 g broccoli florets (2 heads)
   1 cup water

   …when timer rings for chicken and rice… Bring broccoli water to a full boil. Cover and set timer for 3 minutes… …or microwave at high using a microwave-safe dish with cover for 3 minutes.

   You may want to steam the broccoli a little longer if you don't like your veggies firm. Toss with butter if you must.

   butter (optional)

   While the broccoli is cooking, I like to take the thighs and turn them to coat the tops in the sauce again. Flip them back to smooth side up when serving on the plate, they look juicier that way. The sauce is supposed to be runny and is amaaaazing on the rice!

   <u>Serves 4-6</u>

DINNER IS READY IN 45 MINUTES

Equipment List:

Oven-safe pot w/ lid
9"x13" oven-safe baking
   dish or pan
Stove-top pot w/ steamer
   basket
Colander
Cutting board
Flipper
Fork and spoon
Sharp veggie knife
Instant read thermometer
Measuring cups and spoons

Per serving:

Calories	362
Fat	6.0 g
Protein	31.4 g
Carbohydrate	45.2 g
Fiber	1.2 g
Sodium	161 mg

U.S. Food Exchanges:	Cdn. Food Choices:
2 1/2 Starch	3 Carb
4 Meat-lean	4 Meat/Alt

prep crew
- cook rice
- prep chicken
- rinse & trim brocolli
- cook chicken
- cook broccoli

stove-top/oven

15
to
prep

Spinach & Cheese Ravioli in a Maple-Tomato Sauce with Green Beans

Don't change yet! Take out equipment.

Take out ingredients.

1. Fill a large **stove-top** pot with water. Cover and bring to a boil.

water

Combine salsa, pesto and maple syrup together in a small mixing bowl. Set aside.

Maple-Tomato Sauce
1/3 cup salsa
2 Tbsp basil pesto (from a jar)
1 Tbsp maple syrup

Add ravioli to boiling water and **reduce heat** to a medium boil. Set timer according to package directions.

3/4 lb or 350 g spinach and cheese ravioli (found in most deli or dairy sections of your grocery store) approx 4 cups

...meanwhile...

2. Melt butter in a large nonstick electric or stove-top **fry pan** at med-high.
Add beans, lemon pepper and soy sauce.
Toss to coat, then **reduce heat** to med-low.
Stir often, until beans are hot, glazed, a bit crunchy, but tender.

Chef-Style Green Beans
1 tsp butter or olive oil

5 cups green or yellow frozen whole beans (1 lb or 450 g) *I like to blend both.*
1/2 tsp lemon pepper
2 tsp soy sauce, reduced-sodium

...when timer rings for ravioli...

3. Drain ravioli in a colander and let stand.

cooked ravioli

Heat Maple-Tomato Sauce in the pasta pot at medium until hot.
Return ravioli to pot and fold gently until all the ravioli is evenly coated.

prepared Maple-Tomato Sauce

Serve ravioli and sprinkle Parmesan on top.

4 tsp Parmesan cheese, grated

This is a lower calorie meal that doubles easily. You may want to add a little garlic toast if any family members have a bigger appetite.

Serves 4

DINNER IS READY IN 30 MINUTES

Equipment List:

Large nonstick electric or
  stove-top fry pan
Large stove-top pot with lid
Small mixing bowl
Colander
Stirring spoon
Large stirring spoon
Measuring cups and spoons

Per serving:

Calories	373
Fat	11.3 g
Protein	16.1 g
Carbohydrate	54.2 g
Fiber	5.3 g
Sodium	610 mg

U.S. Food Exchanges:	Cdn. Food Choices:
2 1/2 Starch	3 Carb
2 Meat-lean	2 Meat/Alt
1 Vegetable	1 1/2 Fat
1 Fat	

Prep crew

- cook pasta
- prep sauce
- prep green beans
- heat sauce and
  pasta

stove-top

15
to
prep

Savory Pot Roast
with Harvest Veggies

...the night before...
Take out equipment.

1. Combine beef broth, asparagus soup, onion flakes, and spice together in your **slow cooker**. Stir.

Place roast inside center pot of slow cooker and spoon sauce all over top of roast. Cover and leave in **fridge** overnight.

…in the morning…
2. Return covered center pot to the outside of **slow cooker**. Set at **low heat**. It's meant to cook for about 8 hours.

…when you arrive home…
3. Rinse baby potatoes in a colander. Place potatoes and carrots together in a large **stove-top** pot with lid containing enough water to cover the vegetables. Cover and bring to a full boil on high heat. Once boiling, **reduce heat** to a low boil. Set timer for 20 minutes or until veggies are tender. (*...or toss veggies in a little olive oil and roast in a preheated oven at 450° F for 20-25 minutes as shown in photo.*)

...meanwhile...
4. Transfer roast from **slow cooker** to a cutting board and cover with foil.

Stir gravy mix with water in coffee mug. Blend into slow cooker juices using a fork or a whisk until it starts to thicken.
If you like your gravy very thick…you will need to do this step in a stove-top pot at a higher heat.

...when timer rings for vegetables...
5. Drain potatoes and carrots in colander and return to pot.

Take out ingredients.

Sauce for Roast
1 can beef broth, reduced-sodium (10 fl oz or 284 mL)
1 can cream of asparagus soup (10 fl oz or 284 mL)
2 Tbsp onion flakes
1 Tbsp garlic & herb seasoning, salt-free

2-3 lbs or 900-1350 g sirloin or round roast, boneless, trimmed
You can double the size of the roast, without increasing the other ingredients, to have leftovers or great lunch meat.

20 baby potatoes (or cut 4 large)
1 lb or 450 g baby carrots (or 4 large carrots peeled and cut into chunks)

aluminum foil

Gravy Mix
3 Tbsp dry brown gravy mix combined with
3 Tbsp water *I like Bisto.*

This has got to be one of my all time favorite weeknight entertaining meals. Add a great salad and guests will moan and groan and think you've gone all out! My mouth is having a fit!!!!

Serves 4-6

DINNER IS READY IN 35 MINUTES

Equipment List:

...the night before...
Slow cooker
Can opener
Large spoon
Measuring spoons

...when you get home...
Large stove-top pot w/ lid
Colander
Ladle
Stirring spoon
Fork or whisk
Coffee mug
Measuring spoons
Aluminum foil

Per serving:

Calories	399
Fat	11.5 g
Protein	32.5 g
Carbohydrate	41.3 g
Fiber	5.1 g
Sodium	804 mg

U.S. Food Exchanges:	Cdn. Food Choices:
2 Starch	2 Carb
4 Meat-lean	4 1/2 Meat/Alt
1 1/2 Vegetable	1/2 Other

Prep crew
- prep sauce & roast
- prep veggies
- prep gravy mix
- cook roast in slowcooker
- boil or bake veggies
- stir gravy
stove-top/
slowcooker

8

15 to prep

Teriyaki Chicken Toss with Spaghettini Pasta

Don't change yet! Take out equipment.

Take out ingredients.

1. Fill a large **stove-top pot** with water, cover and bring to a boil for pasta.

water

2. Heat oil in large nonstick electric or stove-top **fry pan** or **wok** at medium.

1 tsp canola or olive oil

Cut chicken into bite size pieces and gradually add to pan as you cut. Season and stir until meat is no longer pink. **Increase heat** to medium high.

**3 chicken breasts, boneless, skinless
  (1 lb or 450 g)**
**1/2 tsp original all purpose seasoning,
  salt-free**
1/2 tsp hot chili flakes

Rinse zucchini and peppers. Chop onion, zucchini and peppers into bite size chunks in that order. Add to pan as you chop.
Rinse and slice mushrooms, adding to pan as you slice. Toss occasionally.

1 small zucchini
1/2 green bell pepper
1/2 red bell pepper
1 small onion
10 mushrooms

3. Place pasta in boiling water, stir and cook uncovered. Set timer for 8 minutes or follow package directions.

3/4 lb or 340 g spaghettini pasta

...meanwhile...

4. Add cornstarch to a small bowl or measuring cup. Gradually add soy sauce while stirring so that the cornstarch is smooth, not lumpy. Mix in the honey-garlic sauce and chicken broth. Add to pan of chicken and veggies. Stir and **reduce heat** to low.

<u>Teriyaki Sauce</u>
1 Tbsp cornstarch
2 Tbsp soy sauce, reduced-sodium
1/3 cup honey-garlic sauce (*I like VH brand or make your own* - see page 90)
1/4 cup chicken broth
  (from a 10 fl oz or 284 mL can)

...when timer rings for pasta...

5. **Reduce heat** to medium-low. Rinse the cooked pasta under hot water in a colander. Let drain. Heat the following in the empty pasta pot; remaining chicken broth, curry powder, basil and honey. Stir to combine, then return pasta to pot. Toss pasta to coat in the spiced broth. **Remove from heat.**

<u>Spiced Broth for Pasta</u>
1 cup chicken broth (remaining broth from can)
2 tsp curry powder
1/2 tsp basil leaves
1 Tbsp liquid honey

Seriously yummy! This means yet another awesome dinner is ready to serve!

<u>Serves 4-6</u>

DINNER IS READY IN 30 MINUTES

Equipment List:

Large nonstick electric or
  stove-top fry pan or wok
Large stove-top pot w/ lid
Small mixing bowl
Colander
2 cutting boards
Sharp meat knife
Sharp veggie knife
Pasta fork
Can opener
2 stirring spoons
Measuring cups and spoons

Per serving:

Calories	372
Fat	2.3 g
Protein	25.0 g
Carbohydrate	62.7 g
Fiber	1.5 g
Sodium	444 mg

U.S. Food Exchanges:	Cdn. Food Choices:
3 1/2 Starch	4 Carb
2 1/2 Meat extra-lean	3 1/2 Meat/Alt
1/2 Other	

prep crew
- cook pasta
- cut & cook chicken
- cut veggies
- prep sauce
- toss pasta in broth
Stove-top

20 to prep

TAKE 5

8

About The Recipes

BBQ Southwest Pizza

I'm always trying to come up with new pizza ideas because I know how easy pizza is to make at home. I double up so that I have leftovers for lunch the next day! It's not much extra work to make two different variations so everyone loves what they are getting. This was a hit with our test families. Take 5 - for the veggies.
Vegetarians, use veggie based chicken strips.

Creamy Pesto Shrimp (or Chicken)

Over and over again parents were shocked by their family's reaction to this recipe. If you don't eat shrimp make everything the same but sauté bite s ize pieces of chicken first. The flavor of this dish is addictive, so I suggest you serve your plates and get the rest in the fridge quickly, or portion control may be out of the question!
If you are vegetarian, sauté firm tofu strips until well browned, remove and continue with sauce adding strips later.

Old Fashioned Beef & Tomato Hash

This recipe isn't fancy, but it's quick and it has that certain down home something about it!
If you like things a little spicier add hot chili flakes, like we do.
If you are vegetarian use soy based hamburger instead of ground beef. Cook it a little longer though, so the soy has a chance to absorb the flavors.

Amazing Chicken Stew

This is definitely my favorite chicken stew. This meal-in-one still can please those picky eaters because the chunks are big and easy to pick out. Take 5 - for the veggies.
If you are vegetarian, you can either make this a total veggie stew and have some type of protein on the side or you can throw in chunks of firm tofu or canned mixed beans or lentils then let it simmer in the sauce for a bit.

Chicken Parmesan

When making this recipe, remember it's really important to put the Parmesan on top of the meat before you put the sauce over top. You will finish it up with some more Parmesan later, but you want that Parm flavor to cook right through the meat.
If you are vegetarian this is sooo good with eggplant. My only suggestion is to sprinkle cornflake crumbs over the Parmesan before you put the sauce over top.

On The Menu — Week Nine

BBQ Southwest Pizza with Fresh Veggies

Our Family Rating: 8

Your Family Rating: _____

TAKE 5

Red

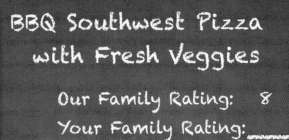

Creamy Pesto Shrimp (or Chicken) with Linguini and Asparagus

Our Family Rating: 10

Your Family Rating: _____

Red

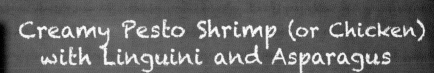

Old Fashioned Beef & Tomato Hash, Mashed Potatoes & Broccoli

Our Family Rating: 8.5

Your Family Rating: _____

Blue

Amazing Chicken Stew on Rice

Our Family Rating: 10

Your Family Rating: _____

TAKE 5

Yellow

Chicken Parmesan with Pasta and Italian Veggies

Our Family Rating: 9.5

Your Family Rating: _____

Green

BBQ Southwest Pizza with Fresh Veggies

Don't change yet! Take out equipment.   **Take out ingredients.**

1. Preheat **oven** to 375° F.

   Heat oil in a large nonstick electric or
   stove-top **fry pan** at medium. Cut meat into bite
   size pieces, adding to pan as you cut. Add spice
   and garlic while meat is browning. When meat
   is no longer pink, set aside on plate.

   1 tsp canola oil
   2 chicken breasts, boneless, skinless
     (3/4 lb or 340 g)
   1 tsp cumin, ground
   1 tsp chili powder
   1 tsp fresh garlic (from a jar)

   Sliver onion, adding to uncleaned pan as you
   sliver. Sliver peppers, adding to pan as you cut.
   Add salsa, Worcestershire sauce and vinegar
   to pan. Stir to combine and simmer until thick.
   Remove from heat.

   <u>**Pizza Veggies**</u>
   1 onion
   1/2 green bell pepper
   1/2 red bell pepper
   1/2 cup chunky salsa (mild, medium or hot)
   1 Tbsp Worcestershire sauce
   1 Tbsp balsamic vinegar

   Brush pizza base with olive oil. Layer in this
   order: pizza veggies, cooked chicken, then
   cover with cheese.

   12" thin crust pizza base (1/2 lb or 225 g)
   2 tsp olive oil, extra-virgin
   prepared pizza veggies
   precooked chicken
   1 cup mozzarella cheese, part-skim,
     shredded

   Place in preheated **oven**. Set timer for 8 minutes
   or until cheese has melted.

   …while pizza is baking…
2. Rinse and cut fresh veggies into large bite-size
   pieces. Arrange on serving plate or serve in the
   colander, as shown.

   <u>**Fresh Veggies**</u>
   3 celery ribs
   2 cups baby carrots
   1/4 head cauliflower or broccoli
   1 red bell pepper
     (or use precut veggies from produce dept)
   ranch dressing, fat-free, for dip (optional)

   …when timer rings for pizza...
3. Remove pizza from oven.
   Drizzle with BBQ sauce and sour cream.
   Sliver lettuce and sprinkle on top as a garnish.

   1 Tbsp southwest BBQ sauce
     (purchase or make your own, see page 94)
   2 Tbsp sour cream, light or fat-free
   2 Romaine lettuce leaves
     (or sliver green leaves from mixed greens)
   tomato (optional)
   green onion (optional)

   *If I have the time, I also cut up tomato and
   green onion and sprinkle that on top too!*

   <u>**Serves 4**</u>

Equipment List:

Large nonstick electric or
  stove-top fry pan
Colander
2 cutting boards
Sharp veggie knife
Sharp meat knife
Stirring spoon
Cheese grater
Pastry brush
Spoon
Plate
Measuring cups and spoons

Per serving:

Calories	482
Fat	14.4 g
Protein	37.3 g
Carbohydrate	53.7 g
Fiber	9.0 g
Sodium	928 mg

U.S. Food Exchanges:	Cdn. Food Choices:
2 Starch	2 Carb
4 1/2 Meat	5 Meat/Alt
1 Other	1 Other

prep crew
- cut & cook chicken
- cut & cook pizza
  veggies
- assemble
- cut fresh veggies

stove-top/oven

TAKE 5

15 to prep

9

Creamy Pesto Shrimp (or Chicken) with Linguini and Asparagus

Don't change yet! Take out equipment.	**Take out ingredients.**

1. Fill a large **stove-top** pot with water and bring to a boil.

water

<u>White Sauce</u>
1 Tbsp butter
1 Tbsp olive oil, extra-virgin
2 Tbsp flour
2 cups 1% milk
1/2 tsp pepper

2. Heat butter and olive oil in a large nonstick electric or stove-top **fry pan** at med-low. **Remove from heat** and whisk in flour. Slowly whisk in milk until smooth. Return to med-low heat. Season with pepper. Heat through while whisking. **Reduce heat** to low.

3. Place pasta in boiling water. Stir. Set timer for 10 minutes or follow package directions.

12 oz or 340 g linguini pasta *I like to put a drop of olive oil in the boiling water. I find it helps the pasta to stay separated.*

   …meanwhile….
4. Whisk cheese into White Sauce until well combined. Blend in pesto.
   If the sauce gets too thick it's OK to keep adding a little bit of milk at a time.
   Fold shrimp into sauce and heat through.

2/3 cup Parmesan cheese, grated, light
1/4 cup basil pesto
milk 1% (optional)

1 lb or 450 g large shrimp, cooked peeled and deveined (or use precooked chicken)

5. Snap off bottom nodes of asparagus and discard. *See page 35.* Rinse in colander or steamer basket. Place water in the bottom of a **stove-top** pot and bring to a full boil with the asparagus in the basket above. Cover and set timer for 4 minutes…
   …or microwave in a microwave-safe dish with cover for 4 minutes.
   …when timer rings for asparagus...
   Drain water. Return to pot with butter.

20 asparagus spears (1 lb or 450 g)
   (or broccoli)
1 cup water

1 tsp butter (optional)

   …when timer rings for pasta…
6. Rinse pasta in colander and return to pot, **no heat**.

Serve shrimp and sauce over linguini.
I like hot chili flakes sprinkled on mine.

hot chili flakes (optional)

<u>Serves 4-6</u>

Equipment List:

Large stove-top pot
Large nonstick electric or
  stove-top fry pan
Stove-top pot w/ steamer
  basket
Colander
Whisk
Stirring spoon
Measuring cups and spoons

Per serving:

Calories	431
Fat	13.5 g
Protein	31.3 g
Carbohydrate	45.8 g
Fiber	2.5 g
Sodium	487 mg

U.S. Food Exchanges:	Cdn. Food Choices:
2 Starch	3 Carb
3 Meat-lean	3 Meat/Alt
1 Fat	1 Fat
1 Milk-low fat	

prep crew
- prep white sauce
  with cheese and pesto
- cook pasta
- prep asparagus
- cook asparagus
- no cutting
  or chopping

Stove-top

15 to prep

9

Old Fashioned Beef & Tomato Hash, Mashed Potatoes and Broccoli

Don't change yet! Take out equipment.

Take out ingredients.

1. Rinse potatoes.
   Cut potatoes into quarters and place in a large **stove-top** pot filled with enough cold water to cover potatoes. Bring to a boil then **reduce heat** to a low boil. Set timer for 10 minutes.

4 large thin skin potatoes (2 lbs or 900 g)
Thin skin Yukon potatoes save you the job of peeling.
water

   …meanwhile…

2. Brown ground beef in a large nonstick electric or stove-top **fry pan** at med-high.
   Stir occasionally.
   When meat is no longer pink, stir in tomatoes (with juice), corn, onion flakes and spices.
   Reduce heat to low stirring occasionally.

1 1/2 lbs or 675 g ground beef, extra-lean

1 can Italian stewed tomatoes
   (19 fl oz or 540 mL)
1 cup frozen corn
   I like the Peaches & Cream variety.
2 Tbsp onion flakes
1 tsp dried dill
1 tsp chipotle seasoning
1 tsp garlic & herb seasoning, salt-free

3. Trim broccoli then rinse in colander or steamer basket. Place water in the bottom of a stove-top pot and bring to a full boil with the broccoli in the basket above. Cover and set timer for 3 minutes...
   ...or microwave at high using a microwave-safe dish with cover for 3 minutes. Let stand.
   Add butter if you must.

1 lb or 450 g broccoli florets (2 heads)
1 cup water

butter (optional)

   …when timer rings for potatoes…

4. Drain potatoes and return to pot, **no heat**.
   Add butter, milk and spice. Mash until smooth with a hand masher or electric beaters.

1 Tbsp butter
1/4 cup 1% milk
1/2 tsp table blend seasoning, salt-free
1/2 tsp dried parsley

I like to smoosh my potatoes and meat together on my plate. My kids like it separate. Either way it's a simple, delicious, down home meal.

<u>**Serves 4-6**</u>

Equipment List:

Large stove-top pot
Large nonstick electric or
  stove-top fry pan
Stove-top pot w/ steamer
  basket
Potato masher or electric
  beaters
Cutting board
Sharp veggie knife
Veggie peeler
Stirring spoon
Can opener
Measuring cups and spoons

Per serving:

Calories	370
Fat	8.6 g
Protein	31.8 g
Carbohydrate	44.1 g
Fiber	5.2 g
Sodium	327 mg

U.S. Food Exchanges:	Cdn. Food Choices:
2 Starch	2 Carb
3 1/2 Meat-lean	3 1/2 Meat/Alt
1 Vegetable	1/2 Other Carb

prep crew
- cut & cook
  potatoes
- cook meat & sauce
- rinse, trim &
  cook broccoli

stove-top

20
to
prep

Amazing Chicken Stew on Rice

Don't change yet! Take out equipment.

Take out ingredients.

1. Combine rice and water in a large microwave-safe pot with lid. Place a paper towel under the pot. **Microwave** at high 8 minutes, then medium 8 minutes. Leave in microwave until ready to serve.

1 1/2 cups basmati or white rice
3 cups water
paper towel

2. Spray a large heavy **stove-top** pot or a nonstick electric fry pan with cooking spray. Heat at medium.
    Cut chicken into bite size pieces and add to pot as you cut. **Increase heat** slightly to med-high. Toss until meat is no longer pink.

cooking spray

3 chicken breasts, boneless, skinless
** (1 lb or 450 g)**

Add spices and Worcestershire sauce. Stir.

1/4 tsp fresh pepper
1/4 tsp garlic and herb seasoning, salt-free
1 tsp lemon pepper
2 tsp Worcestershire sauce

Rinse celery and mushrooms.
Chop onion, slice celery and mushrooms using a different knife and cutting board.
Add to pot as you cut.

3 celery ribs
12 mushrooms
1 onion

Rinse broccoli and carrots in a colander.
Add to pot.

Add soup and gradually stir in water.

3 cups frozen broccoli florets, or use fresh
** (3/4 lb or 340 g)**
2 cups frozen baby carrots (1/2 lb or 225 g)
1 can cream of chicken soup, reduced-
** sodium (10 fl oz or 284 mL)**
1 cup water

...when stew starts to boil...
Reduce heat to low and simmer until hot and flavors have combined (approx 5-10 minutes). Check to make sure you can pierce the carrot easily with a fork.

I love serving my stew over top of the rice but my kids like scooping it together side by side! this simple but delicious stew will be a family favorite!

<u>**Serves 6**</u>

Equipment List:

Large microwave-safe pot
  w/ lid
Large heavy stove-top pot
  or nonstick electric fry pan
Colander
2 cutting boards
Sharp meat knife
Sharp veggie knife
Large stirring spoon
Ladle
Can opener
Fork
Measuring cups and spoons
Paper towel

Per serving:

Calories	351
Fat	3.4 g
Protein	26.0 g
Carbohydrate	54.4 g
Fiber	6.2 g
Sodium	431 mg

U.S. Food Exchanges:	Cdn. Food Choices:
2 1/2 Starch	3 Carb
3 Meat-lean	4 Meat/Alt
2 Vegetable	

prep crew
- prep & cook rice
- cut chicken
- rinse & cut
  veggies
- cook stew

stove-top/
microwave

TAKE 5

20 to prep

9

Chicken Parmesan
with Pasta and Italian Veggies

Don't change yet! Take out equipment.

Take out ingredients.

1. Preheat **oven** to **375º F**.
   Place chicken breasts in a large lasagna or
   cake pan. Sprinkle with Parmesan cheese.
   Pour pasta sauce evenly over the top.

   Cover with aluminum foil and place in
   preheated oven. Set timer for 35 minutes.

**4 boneless skinless chicken breasts, or 10
thighs (1 1/2 lbs or 675 g)**
1/4 cup Parmesan cheese, light, grated
1 can tomato pasta sauce
  (24 fl oz or 680 mL)
  (choose a lower sodium brand)
aluminum foil

Use the veggies below or use leftover cold
veggies from your pizza meal.

…meanwhile…

2. Rinse baby carrots and grape tomatoes. Place
   in a salad bowl. Rinse, then slice cucumber
   into chunks adding to salad bowl as you cut.
   Rinse, then quarter mushrooms adding to bowl
   as you cut. Cut onion into small chunks and
   add to bowl. Drizzle with dressing and toss to
   coat. Set aside in **fridge** for dinner or serve as
   an appetizer.

1 cup baby carrots
1 cup grape tomatoes
1 English cucumber
5 mushrooms
1/8 red onion (optional)
2 Tbsp Italian dressing, light

…when timer rings for chicken…

3. Leave chicken in the oven. *The timer was just
   to remind you it's time to start cooking the
   pasta. (Chicken cooks for about 55 minutes.)*
   Fill a large **stove-top** pot with water and bring
   to a boil for pasta.
   Add pasta to boiling water. Set timer for 11
   minutes or follow package directions.

water

3 cups penne pasta

…when timer rings for pasta…
   Rinse pasta in a colander under hot water.
   Return to pot and toss with basil and olive oil.

1 tsp basil leave
1 tsp olive oil, extra-virgin

4. Remove chicken from **oven** and sprinkle
   cheeses over top. Return to oven and reset
   timer for 5 minutes or until cheese is melted.

   Serve chicken on top of pasta or on the side.

**1 1/2 cups mozzarella cheese, part-skim,
  shredded**
2 Tbsp Parmesan cheese, light, grated

Serves 4-6

DINNER IS READY IN 60 MINUTES

Equipment List:

Large lasagna or cake pan
Large stove-top pot
Cutting board
Colander
Salad bowl
2 stirring spoons
Sharp veggie knife
Can opener
Measuring cups and spoons
Aluminum foil

Per serving:

Calories	532
Fat	10.3 g
Protein	45.3 g
Carbohydrate	61.4 g
Fiber	6.2 g
Sodium	717 mg

U.S. Food Exchanges:	Cdn. Food Choices:
3 Starch	3 Carb
5 Meat v-lean	5 Meat/Alt
3 Vegetable	1 Other Carb

prep crew
- assemble
- cut veggies
- cook pasta

stove-top/oven

15 to prep

9

About The Recipes

Lean Mean Shepherd's Pie

Our test families go gaga over this shepherd's pie! If you have a small family leftovers freeze beautifully.

Veggie grind works great if you like it meat free.

Thai Chicken Wraps

This meal is so fun. It's often a movie night meal for our family. It suits a sophisticated palate, but it's fun like take-out.

Take 5 - for the veggies and/or chicken.

Vegetarians, this is an easy one: soak some tofu in the dressing first, then make the wraps with all the veggies you like. Crushed peanuts are great too!

Taco Pasta

Over the years I have heard mixed reviews on chili. For some it's a family favorite and others not so much. I experimented to see if it was the flavor or if it was the texture of the beans that was the turn off. Hands down, it was the texture, so I kept the flavor, made it into a pasta sauce and served it with broccoli. Voila! A major hit with all the test families.

This is amazing with veggie grind if you are vegetarian.

Chili-Lime Chicken

This recipe was a 10 out of 10 for most test families. One of our testers pointed out it's important to simmer the sauce on low like the recipe says, or you lose out on the nummy sauce.

For vegetarians, fry up firm tofu until crisp, remove from pan, add sauce to pan, then put tofu back in the sauce.

Crustless Quiche

A lot of people like quiche, but not a lot of people want to bother with crust, especially not in the work week. This is a great way to get the best of both worlds. What I also love about quiche is that you can make it anything you want, similar to pizza. With or without meat, this dish served with salad is one my personal favorites.

On The Menu - Week Ten

Lean Mean Shepherd's Pie with Baby Peas

Our Family Rating: 9.5

Your Family Rating: _____

Blue

Thai Chicken Wraps

Our Family Rating: 10

Your Family Rating: _____

TAKE 5

Yellow

Taco Pasta with Broccoli

Our Family Rating: 10

Your Family Rating: _____

Red

Chili-Lime Chicken with Rice, Zucchini & Mushrooms

Our Family Rating: 10

Your Family Rating: _____

Yellow

Crustless Quiche with Spinach Salad

Our Family Rating: 9.5

Your Family Rating: _____

TAKE

Blue

Lean Mean Shepherd's Pie with Baby Peas

Don't change yet! Take out equipment.

Take out ingredients.

1. Preheat **oven** to 375º F.

2. Rinse potatoes and cut into quarters. Place in a **stove-top** pot and cover with cold water. Bring to a boil, then **reduce heat** to medium. Set timer for 10 minutes.

4 large thin skin potatoes (2 lbs or 900 g) (or 8 medium)
water

...while potatoes come to a boil...
3. Brown meat with spice in a large nonstick electric or stove-top **fry pan** or wok, at med-high, until meat is no longer pink. **Remove from heat**. Add ketchup, spice and Worcestershire sauce to cooked meat. Stir well. Pour Meat Mixture into a large **oven-safe** pan or casserole dish.

<u>Meat Mixture</u>
2 lbs or 900 g ground beef, extra-lean
2/3 cup ketchup
1 1/2 tsp original all purpose seasoning, salt-free
2 1/2 tsp Worcestershire sauce

Rinse frozen corn in a colander and spread it evenly over the Meat Mixture.
Spread creamed corn over the frozen corn.

1 cup Peaches & Cream style corn, frozen
1 can cream style corn (14 fl oz or 398 mL)

...when timer rings for potatoes...
Potatoes are ready if you can easily pierce through it with a knife. If not they need a few more minutes, then **remove from heat**. Drain potatoes in a colander then return to pot. Add butter and milk. Mash with a hand masher or electric beaters. Top casserole with mashed potatoes using a fork to spread. Bake in **oven** uncovered for 25 minutes.

1 tsp butter
1/4 cup 1% milk

...meanwhile...
4. Rinse peas in colander or steamer basket. Place water in the bottom of a **stove-top** pot and place peas in the basket above. Cover and let stand, **no heat**.

4 cups frozen peas (1 1/3 lbs or 600 g)
1 cup water

...when timer rings for Shepherd's Pie...
Heat peas at high. When you can see steam, set timer for 3 minutes...
...or microwave on high in a microwave-safe dish with cover for 3 minutes.
Toss with butter if you must.
Take the Shepherd's Pie out, and let stand for about 5 minutes before serving.

We like to broil the top for 2-3 minutes so the potatoes get a little crunchy!

1 tsp butter (optional)

<u>Serves 6-8</u>

BLUE

150

DINNER IS READY IN 55 MINUTES

Equipment List:

Large stove-top pot
Large nonstick electric or
    stove-top fry pan or wok
Large oven-safe pan or
    casserole dish
Stove-top pot w/ steamer
    basket
Colander
Hand masher or electric
    beaters
Can opener
Sharp veggie knife
Mixing spoon
Spoon for spreading
Knife and fork
Measuring cups and spoon

Per serving:

Calories	425
Fat	13.3 g
Protein	29.0 g
Carbohydrate	50.3 g
Fiber	6.7 g
Sodium	552 mg

U.S. Food Exchanges:	Cdn. Food Choices:
2 1/2 Starch	3 Carb
4 Meat-lean	4 Meat/Alt
1/2 Other	

Prep crew
- boil potatoes
- brown meat
- prep meat base
- mash potatoes
- assemble
- prep peas
- cook peas

stove-top/oven

20 to prep

Thai Chicken Wraps

Don't change yet! Take out equipment.

Take out ingredients.

1. Fill a **kettle** with water and bring to a boil on high heat for noodles.

water

2. Heat oil in a large nonstick electric or stove-top **fry pan** at medium heat. Cut chicken into small bite-size pieces, adding to pan as you cut. Stir until meat is no longer pink. Cover and **remove from heat**.

1 tsp sesame oil
3 chicken breasts, boneless, skinless
  (1 lb or 450 g)

3. Place noodles in a small pot and completely cover with boiling water from **kettle**. Set timer according to package insructions (about 3-5 minutes).
   ...when timer rings for noodles...
   Drain in a colander and rinse under very cold water. Set aside.

1/4 lb or 113 g rice stick or vermicelli
  noodles
boiling water

very cold water

   ....meanwhile...
4. Soften peanut butter in **microwave** for 10 seconds in a microwave-safe bowl. Whisk in sweet chili sauce, ginger powder, garlic, lime juice, rice vinegar, soy sauce, and sweet chili sauce. Set aside.

<u>Thai Wrap Sauce</u>
1/4 cup peanut butter, light
1/2 cup sweet Thai chili sauce
  (found in Asian foods) for a less spicy
  version, replace with Catalina salad dressing
1 tsp ginger, ground
1 tsp fresh garlic (from a jar)
2 tsp lime juice
2 tsp rice vinegar (can be seasoned)
2 tsp soy sauce, reduced-sodium

5. Rinse lettuce in basket of salad spinner and spin dry.
   Peel carrots and cut into tiny, long narrow sticks or use a julienne peeler.
   Rinse cucumber and do the same.
   Rinse and sliver red pepper.
   Rinse bean sprouts.

1/4 head green leaf lettuce or bagged lettuce

2 large carrots (*Now you can find these
  already cut julienne style!*)
1/2 English cucumber
1 red bell pepper
1/2 lb or 225 g bean sprouts (optional)

6. Lay tortillas on plate. Layer with lettuce and noodles.
   Add chicken, then drizzle with Thai wrap sauce. Top with cut carrots, cucumber, red pepper and bean sprouts. *Fantastic!*

6 whole wheat or flour tortillas, 10"
  (choose a lower sodium brand)
Replace tortillas with rice wraps if you prefer.
reserved noodles

<u>Serves 4-6</u>

DINNER IS READY IN 30 MINUTES

Equipment List:

Large nonstick electric or
    stove-top fry pan
Small pot
Microwave-safe bowl
Colander
2 cutting boards
Kettle
Salad spinner
Sharp meat knife
Sharp veggie knife
Peeler for carrots
Whisk
Mixing spoons
Measuring cups and spoons

Per serving:

Calories	475
Fat	9.9 g
Protein	27.0 g
Carbohydrate	69.9 g
Fiber	4.2 g
Sodium	712 mg

U.S. Food Exchanges:	Cdn. Food Choices:
3 1/2 Starch	4 Carb
2 Meat-lean	2 Meat/Alt
2 Vegetable	1 Fat
1 Fat	

prep crew
- prep noodles
- cut & cook chicken
- prep thai sauce
- cut veggies
- assemble

Stove-top/electric
fry pan

TAKE 5

20 to prep

10

Taco Pasta with Broccoli

Don't change yet! Take out equipment.

1. Fill a large **stove-top** pot with water. Cover and bring to a boil at high heat for pasta.

2. Heat oil in a large nonstick electric or stove-top **fry pan** at medium. Dice onion, adding to pan as you cut. Cook, stirring occasionally, until caramelized. Add beef and spices to fry pan. Break up the beef with a spoon stirring occasionally. Brown until no longer pink.

    Add pasta sauce and broth to cooked meat and stir. **Reduce heat** to low.

3. Place pasta into boiling water and set timer for 2 minutes less than package directions (approx 8 minutes).

4. Trim broccoli then rinse in colander or steamer basket. Place water in the bottom of a stove-top pot with the broccoli in the basket above. Cover and let stand **no heat**.

    ...when timer rings for pasta...
5. Rinse pasta under hot water in a colander. Add pasta to meat pan gently folding into sauce to heat through.

6. Heat broccoli at high until you see steam. Set timer for 3 minutes or until broccoli is firm but tender...
    ...or microwave at high using a microwave-safe dish with cover for 3 minutes.

    Add a little butter to broccoli if you must.

    We love grated Parmesan on the pasta. We put hot chili flakes on the table for those who like it spicier!

Take out ingredients.

water

Taco Pasta Sauce
1 tsp canola oil
1 onion

1 lb or 450 g ground beef, extra-lean
2 tsp chili powder
1 tsp cumin
1/8 tsp turmeric

1 can tomato pasta sauce
  (24 fl oz or 680 mL) *I like to use spicy.*
  (choose a lower sodium brand)
1 cup beef broth, reduced-sodium
  (or use all 10 fl oz or 284 mL can)
  You can use chicken broth if on hand.

3 cups bow tie pasta

1 lb or 450 g broccoli florets (2 heads)
1 cup water

butter (optional)

Parmesan, grated, light (optional)
hot chili flakes (optional)

Serves 6

DINNER IS READY IN 30 MINUTES

Equipment List:

Large stove-top pot w/ lid
Large nonstick electric or
  stove-top fry pan
Cutting board
Colander
Stove-top pot w/ steamer
  basket
Sharp veggie knife
Stirring spoon
Can opener
Measuring cups and spoons

Per serving:

Calories	426
Fat	10.8 g
Protein	25.2 g
Carbohydrate	56.0 g
Fiber	4.5 g
Sodium	449 mg

U.S. Food Exchanges:	Cdn. Food Choices:
3 Starch	3 1/2 Carb
2 1/2 Meat-lean	3 1/2 Meat/Alt
1 Fat	
1 Vegetable	

prep crew
- cut onion
- brown and spice meat
- undercook pasta
- assemble
- rinse and prep broccoli
- cook broccoli

stove-top

15 to prep

Chili-Lime Chicken with Rice, Zucchini & Mushrooms

Don't change yet! Take out equipment.

1. Combine rice and water in a large microwave-safe pot with lid. Place a paper towel under the pot. **Microwave** at high 8 minutes, then medium 8 minutes.

   ...meanwhile...

2. Heat oil in a large nonstick electric or stove-top **fry pan** or wok at medium.

   Cut chicken into bite-size pieces and add to pan as you cut. Stir until no longer pink.

   Add ginger, garlic and pepper to pan and stir. Add lime juice, brown sugar, sweet chili sauce and water to the pan and stir.

   You might have to increase the heat to medium high as you want the sauce to thicken up a little. You do want it a bit runny though 'cause it's great with the rice!

   ...when timer rings for rice...

3. Lift rice with a fork, cover and let stand for another 5 minutes. *Careful it's hot!*

   …while chicken is simmering...

4. Heat oil in another large nonstick electric or stove top **fry pan** or wok on medium. Rinse and cut zucchini and mushrooms into large chunks adding to pan as you cut. Add spice and stir. Cook until tender but crisp.

   Serve the chicken and sauce directly on the rice or on the side. This is really simple yet the flavor will knock your socks off!

Take out ingredients.

1 1/2 cups basmati or white rice
3 cups water
paper towel

1 Tbsp sesame oil

4 chicken breasts, boneless, skinless
  (1 1/3 lbs or 600 g)

1 1/2 Tbsp fresh ginger (from a jar)
  or 1 1/2 tsp ground ginger
1 Tbsp fresh garlic (from a jar)
  or 3 cloves minced
1/4 tsp pepper
1/4 cup lime juice
3 Tbsp brown sugar
1-2 Tbsp sweet Thai chili sauce
  (depending on spice peference)
2/3 cup water

1 tsp olive or sesame oil

2 small zucchini
10 mushrooms
1/2 tsp garlic and herb seasoning, salt-free

<u>**Serves 4-6**</u>

DINNER IS READY IN 30 MINUTES

Equipment List:

2 large nonstick electric or
   stove-top fry pans or woks
Large microwave-safe pot
   w/ lid
2 cutting boards
Sharp meat knife
Sharp veggie knife
2 stirring spoons
Fork
Measuring cups and spoons
Paper towel

Per serving:

Calories	349
Fat	5.0 g
Protein	27.9 g
Carbohydrate	47.3 g
Fiber	2.0 g
Sodium	104 mg

U.S. Food Exchanges:	Cdn. Food Choices:
3 Starch	3 Carb
2 1/2 Meat v-lean	2 1/2 Meat/Alt

prep crew
- cook rice
- cut chicken
- brown chicken
- prep chili lime sauce
- rinse veggies
- cut and cook veggies

stove-top

20
to
prep

Crustless Quiche with Spinach Salad

Don't change yet! Take out equipment.

Take out ingredients.

1. Preheat **oven** to **375° F**.
Add butter and oil to a large nonstick electric or stove-top **fry pan** over medium heat. Dice onion and add to pan as you chop. Sauté until just translucent stirring occasionally. **Remove from heat.**

1 tsp butter
1 Tbsp olive oil, extra-virgin
1/3 cup onion (1/4 of an onion)

Chop broccoli into small bite size pieces and add to onion pan, **no heat**. Slice mushrooms and add to pan. Add whatever else you like. *I love zucchini, tomato and even shrimp. The sky's the limit...as long as it fits in the pan!*

<u>Vegetable Mixture</u>
1/2 cup broccoli florets (or any other green veggie you have on hand)
4 mushrooms
1/2 cup zucchini (optional)
1 Roma tomato (optional)
1 cup shrimp, cooked, deveined (optional)

Separate eggs. Put whites in a medium size bowl and yolks in cup. Whisk egg whites until frothy. Add yolks, cream, milk, biscuit mix and pepper. Whisk together until well blended.

<u>Egg Mixture</u>
4 large eggs (whites first)
1/4 cup 10% cream
3/4 cup 1% milk
1/2 cup biscuit mix *I like Bisquick.*
1/4 tsp fresh ground pepper

Spray a 10 inch pie plate (glass is best) with cooking spray. Pour egg mixture into pie plate. Sprinkle vegetable mixture into egg mixture.

cooking spray

Grate cheeses and sprinkle over egg mixture. Bake in preheated **oven** on lower rack. Set timer for 40 minutes or until top is golden brown and inserted knife comes out clean.

1/4 cup gruyere cheese (or Parmesan)
1/4 cup mozzarella cheese, part-skim, shredded
1/2 cup cheddar cheese, light, grated

...while Quiche is cooking...

2. Rinse spinach in basket of salad spinner, spin dry and place on dinner plates. Sliver pepper and red onion. Layer these over the spinach. Sprinkle with blueberries and nuts if you like. Drizzle with your favorite dressing.

1 bag baby spinach (6 oz or 170 g)
1/4 red bell pepper
1/8 red onion
1/2 cup frozen wild blueberries
2 Tbsp matchstick almonds
1/4 cup fruit vinaigrette, light (or your favorite dressing)

Ketchup or HP sauce allowed!

<u>Serves 4</u>

Equipment List:

Large nonstick electric or
  stove-top fry pan
9" pie plate (glass is best)
Medium mixing bowl
Salad spinner
Salad tongs
Individual serving plates
Cutting board
Sharp veggie knife
Whisk
Cheese grater
Flipper
Stirring spoon
Measuring cups and spoons

Per serving:

Calories	379
Fat	22.7 g
Protein	19.3 g
Carbohydrate	24.4 g
Fiber	2.8 g
Sodium	537 mg

U.S. Food Exchanges:	Cdn. Food Choices:
1 Starch	1 Carb
3 1/2 meat-lean	3 1/2 Meat/Alt
1/2 Fat	1/2 Fat

prep crew
- cut veggies
- saute onion
- assemble quiche
- cut & prep salad

stove-top/oven

TAKE 5

20 to prep

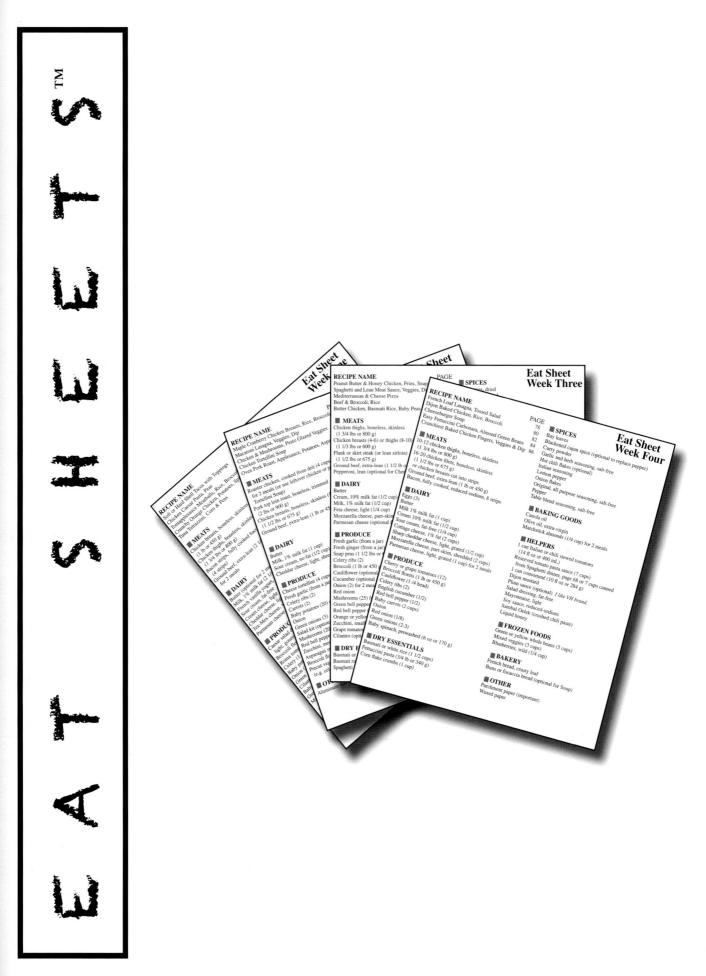

EAT SHEETS™

Eat Sheet Week Three

Eat Sheet Week Four

RECIPE NAME
French Loaf Lasagna, Tossed Salad
Dijon Baked Chicken, Rice, Broccoli
Cheeseburger Soup
Easy Fettuccini Carbonara, Almond Green Beans
Crunchiest Baked Chicken Fingers, Veggies & Dip

PAGE
78
80
82
84
86

■ **SPICES**
Bay leaves
Blackened cajun spice (optional to replace pepper)
Curry powder
Garlic and herb seasoning, salt-free
Hot chili flakes (optional)
Italian seasoning
Lemon pepper
Onion flakes
Original, all purpose seasoning, salt-free
Pepper
Table blend seasoning, salt-free

■ **BAKING GOODS**
Canola oil
Olive oil, extra-virgin
Matchstick almonds (1/4 cup) for 2 meals

■ **HELPERS**
1 can Italian or chili stewed tomatoes
    (14 fl oz or 400 mL.)
Reserved tomato pasta sauce (7 cups)
    from Spaghetti dinner, page 68 or 7 cups canned
1 can consommé (10 fl oz or 284 g)
Dijon mustard
Plum sauce (optional) *I like VH brand.*
Salad dressing, fat-free
Mayonnaise, light
Soy sauce, reduced-sodium
Sambal Oelek (crushed chili paste)
Liquid honey

■ **FROZEN FOODS**
Green or yellow whole beans (5 cups)
Mixed veggies (3 cups)
Blueberries, wild (1/4 cup)

■ **BAKERY**
French bread, crusty loaf
Buns or focaccia bread (optional for Soup)

■ **OTHER**
Parchment paper (important)
Waxed paper

RECIPE NAME
Peanut Butter & Honey Chicken, Fries, Snap
Spaghetti and Lean Meat Sauce, Veggies, D
Mediterranean & Cheese Pizza
Beef & Broccoli, Rice
Butter Chicken, Basmati Rice, Baby Peas

■ **MEATS**
Chicken thighs, boneless, skinless
    (1 3/4 lbs or 800 g)
Chicken breasts (4-6) or thighs (8-10)
    (1 1/3 lbs or 600 g)
Flank or skirt steak (or lean sirloin)
    (1 1/2 lbs or 675 g)
Ground beef, extra-lean (1 1/2 lb o
Pepperoni, lean (optional for Chee

■ **MEATS**
10-12 chicken thighs, boneless, skinless
    (1 3/4 lbs or 800 g)
16-20 chicken filets, boneless, skinless
    (1 1/2 lbs or 675 g)
or chicken breasts cut into strips
Ground beef, extra-lean (1 lb or 450 g)
Bacon, fully cooked, reduced-sodium, 8 strips

■ **DAIRY**
Butter
Cream, 10% milk fat (1/2 cup)
Milk, 1% milk fat (1/2 cup)
Feta cheese, light (1/4 cup)
Mozzarella cheese, part-skim
Parmesan cheese (optional

■ **DAIRY**
Eggs (3)
Butter
Milk 1% milk fat (1 cup)
Cream 10% milk fat (1/2 cup)
Sour cream, fat-free (1/4 cup)
Cottage cheese, 1% fat (2 cups)
Sharp cheddar cheese, light, grated (1/2 cup)
Mozzarella cheese, part-skim, shredded (2 cups)
Parmesan cheese, light, grated (1 cup) for 2 meals

■ **PRODUCE**
Fresh garlic (from a jar)
Fresh ginger (from a jar
Snap peas (1 1/2 lbs or
Celery ribs (2)
Broccoli (1 lb or 450
Cauliflower (optional
Cucumber (optional
Onion (2) for 2 meal
Red onion
Mushrooms (25)
Green bell pepper
Red bell pepper
Orange or yello
Zucchini, small
Cilantro (opti

■ **PRODUCE**
Cherry or grape tomatoes (12)
Broccoli florets (1 lb or 450 g)
Cauliflower (1 /4 head)
Celery ribs (2)
Red bell pepper (1/2)
English cucumber (1/2)
Baby carrots (2 cups)
Onion
Red onion (1/8)
Green onions (2-3)
Baby spinach, prewashed (6 oz or 170 g)

■ **DRY ESSENTIALS**
Basmati or white rice (1 1/2 cups)
Fettuccini pasta (1/4 cup)
Corn flake crumbs (1 cup)

RECIPE NAME
Maple Cranberry Chicken Breasts, Rice, Brocco
Macaroni Lasagna, Veggies, Dip
Chicken & Mushrooms, Pesto Glazed Veggies
Chicken Tortellini Soup
Oven Pork Roast, Applesauce, Potatoes, Asp

■ **MEATS**
Roaster chicken, cooked from deli (4 cups
    for 2 meals (or use leftover chicken or
    Tortellini Soup)
Pork top loin roast, boneless, trimmed
    (2 lbs or 900 g)
Chicken breasts, boneless, skinless
    (1 1/2 lbs or 675 g)
Ground beef, extra-lean (1 lb or 45

■ **DAIRY**
Butter
Milk, 1% milk fat (1 cup)
Sour cream, no-fat (1/2 cup)
Cheddar cheese, light, shre

■ **PRODUCE**
Cheese tortellini (4 cup
Fresh garlic (from a jar
Celery ribs (2)
Carrots (2)
Baby potatoes (20)
Onion
Green onions (3)
Salad kit (option
Mushrooms (20
Red bell peppe
Zucchini, me
Asparagus s
Broccoli flo
Precut veg
    (e.g. ce
Cilan
Bab
Gro

■ **DRY E**
Basmati or
Basmati ri
Spaghetti

RECIPE NAME
Soft or Hard Shell Tacos with Toppings
Chicken Caesar Pasta, Veggies & Dip
Tonapplesauce Meatballs, Rice, Brocco
Crunchy Orange Chicken, Potatoes, S
Tuna Tetrazzini, Corn & Peas

■ **MEATS**
Chicken breasts, boneless, skinless
    (1 lb or 450 g)
Chicken thighs, boneless, skinle
    (1 3/4 lbs or 800 g)
Bacon strips, fully cooked bac
    (4 strips)
Ground beef, extra-lean (2
    for 2 meals

■ **DAIRY**
Butter (optional for 2 m
Milk, 1% milk fat (2 1
French vanilla yogurt
Sour cream, fat-free
Cream cheese, light
Tex-Mex cheese, sh
Parmesan cheese

■ **PRODUCE**
Caesar salad k
light, gourm
French gour
Roma tom
Celery (1
Baby po
Onion
Cilan
Bab
Gro
M

RECIPE NAME

■ MEATS

Chicken breasts, boneless, skinless (3)
  (1 lb or 450 g)
Chicken thighs, boneless, skinless
  (1 3/4 lbs or 800 g)
Bacon strips, fully cooked bacon, low-sodium
  (4 strips)
Ground beef, extra-lean (2 1/2 lbs or 1125 g)
  for 2 meals

■ DAIRY

Butter (optional for 2 meals)
Milk, 1% milk fat (2 1/4 cups) for 2 meals
French vanilla yogurt, low-fat
Sour cream, fat-free or light
Cream cheese, light (5 1/2 oz or 83 g)
Cheddar cheese, light, shredded (3/4 cup)
Tex-Mex cheese, shredded (1 1/2 cups)
Parmesan cheese, light, grated (optional for Pasta)

■ PRODUCE

Caesar salad dressing, garlic lovers,
  light, gourmet, refrigerated (1/2 cup)
Broccoli florets, 2-3 heads (1 lb or 450 g)
Roma tomatoes (4)
Celery ribs (2)
Baby potatoes (20) or 4 large potatoes
Onion (1) for 2 meals
Green onions (4)
Cilantro (optional for Tacos)
Baby spinach, prewashed (6 oz or 170 g)
Green leaf lettuce (1/4 head for Tacos)
Mandarin oranges or oranges (2)

■ OTHER

Aluminum foil
Paper towels

■ SPICES

Chili powder
Cumin powder
Curry powder
Garlic powder
Onion flakes
Onion powder
Original, all purpose seasoning, salt-free
Poppy seeds
Table blend seasoning, salt-free
Turmeric
Pepper

■ BAKING GOODS

Olive oil, extra-virgin
Brown sugar

■ HELPERS

Applesauce, unsweetened (1/2 cup)
Orange juice, unsweetened (1/2 cup)
Liquid honey
Mayonnaise, light
Dijon mustard
Ketchup
Salsa, chunky
Sambal Oelek (crushed chili paste) found in Asian foods
1 can tomato soup (10 fl oz or 284 mL)
1 can cream of mushroom soup, reduced-sodium
  (10 fl oz or 284 mL)
1 can solid tuna in water (6 1/2 oz or 180 g)

■ FROZEN FOODS

Baby peas (5 cups) for 2 meals
Corn, Peaches and Cream style if available (2 cups)

■ DRY ESSENTIALS

Fusilli pasta or any kind of spiral pasta (4 cups)
Vermicelli pasta (12 oz or 340 g)
  (use regular vermicelli or spaghettini, only use rice
    vermicelli if there are wheat allergies in your family)
Basmati or white rice (1 1/2 cups)
Corn flake crumbs (1 cup)

■ BAKERY

Croutons (1/2 cup)
Tortillas, soft (6) flour, multigrain or corn 10"
  (choose a lower sodium brand)

Custom Eat Sheet™

RECIPE NAME   Page

_____

_____

_____

_____

_____

■ MEATS

■ DAIRY

■ PRODUCE

■ DRY ESSENTIALS

■ SPICES

■ BAKING GOODS

■ HELPERS

■ FROZEN FOODS

■ BAKERY

■ OTHER

Eat Sheet™ Week 2

■ MEATS
Roaster chicken, cooked, from deli
  (1 whole chicken or 4 cups meat) for 2 meals
  (or use leftover chicken or pork for Tortellini Soup)
Pork top loin roast, boneless, trimmed
  (2 lbs or 900 g)
Chicken breasts, boneless, skinless (4)
  (1 1/2 lbs or 675 g)
Ground beef, extra-lean (1 lb or 450 g)

■ DAIRY
Butter
Milk, 1% milk fat (1 cup)
Sour cream, fat-free or light (1/2 cup)
Cheddar cheese, light, shredded (2 cups)

■ PRODUCE
Cheese tortellini (12 oz or 350 g) (in deli section)
Fresh garlic (from a jar)
Celery ribs (2)
Carrots (2)
Baby potatoes (20) or 4 large thin-skinned potatoes
Onion
Green onions (3)
Salad kit (optional with Tortellini Soup)
Mushrooms (20) for 2 meals
Red bell pepper (1) & Yellow bell pepper (1)
Zucchini, medium (2)
Asparagus spears (20)
Broccoli florets, 2-3 heads (1 lb or 450 g)
Precut veggies (1 1/2 lbs or 675 g)
  (e.g. celery, cauliflower, broccoli and carrots)

■ OTHER
Aluminum foil
Paper towel

■ SPICES
Celery salt
Cinnamon
Garlic & herb seasoning blend, salt-free
Garlic powder
Hot chili flakes (optional)
Italian seasoning, salt-free
Onion flakes
Original, all purpose seasoning, salt-free
Poultry seasoning
Rosemary leaves
Table blend seasoning, salt free
Salt & pepper

■ BAKING GOODS
Olive oil, extra-virgin
Cooking spray
Canola oil
Apple cider vinegar
Flour
Dry brown gravy mix (I like Bisto)
Maple syrup (1/2 cup)
Cranberries, dried, unsweetened

■ HELPERS
Applesauce, unsweetened (1/2 cup)
Chicken broth, reduced-sodium
  (4 1/2 – 5 cups) for 2 meals
1 can pasta sauce, tomato blend, choose a lower
  sodium brand (24 fl oz or 680 mL)
Worcestershire sauce
Hot sauce (optional for Tortellini Soup)
Basil pesto (from a jar)
Mayonnaise, light

■ FROZEN FOODS
Peas (1 cup)
Peas (1 cup) (optional for Tortellini Soup)
Puff pastry patti shells, 1 pkg of 6 (10 oz or 300 g)
  (can use precooked shells found in bakery section)

■ DRY ESSENTIALS
Basmati or white rice (1 1/4 cups)
Macaroni, whole wheat (2 1/2 cups)

Custom Eat Sheet™

RECIPE NAME   Page

_____

_____

_____

_____

_____

■ MEATS

■ DAIRY

■ PRODUCE

■ DRY ESSENTIALS

■ SPICES

■ BAKING GOODS

■ HELPERS

■ FROZEN FOODS

■ BAKERY

■ OTHER

■ MEATS

Chicken thighs, boneless, skinless
  (1 3/4 lbs or 800 g)
Chicken breasts (4-6) or thighs (8-10), boneless, skinless
  (1 1/3 lbs or 600 g)
Flank or skirt steak (or lean sirloin)
  (1 1/2 lbs or 675 g)
Ground beef, extra-lean (1 1/2 lb or 675 g)
Pepperoni, lean (optional for Cheese Pizza)

■ DAIRY

Butter
Cream, 10% milk fat (1/2 cup)
Milk, 1% milk fat (1/2 cup)
Feta cheese, light (1/4 cup)
Mozzarella cheese, part-skim, shredded (1 1/2 cups)
Parmesan cheese (optional for Spaghetti)

■ PRODUCE

Fresh garlic (from a jar)
Fresh ginger (from a jar)
Snap peas (1 1/2 lbs or 675 g)
Celery ribs (2)
Broccoli (1 lb or 450 g)
Cauliflower (optional for Veggies & Dip)
Cucumber (optional for Veggies & Dip)
Onion, large (2) for 2 meals
Red onion
Mushrooms (27) for 3 meals
Green or red bell pepper (1)
Red, orange or yellow bell pepper (2) for 2 meals
Zucchini, small (2) for 2 meals
Grape tomatoes (12)
Cilantro (optional for Butter Chicken)

■ DRY ESSENTIALS

Basmati or white rice (or quinoa) (1 1/2 cups)
Basmati rice (1 1/2 cups) (for Butter Chicken)
Spaghetti pasta (12 oz or 340 g)

■ SPICES

Basil leaves, dried
Cinammon, ground
Chili powder
Garam masala
Hot chili flakes (optional)
Italian seasoning
Oregano leaves
Paprika
Pepper
Rosemary
Sesame seeds
Thyme leaves

■ BAKING GOODS

Canola oil
Olive oil (optional)
Sesame oil
Brown sugar
Sugar
Pine nuts or matchstick almonds (1 Tbsp for Pizza)

■ HELPERS

Peanut butter, light
Peanut satay sauce
Madras curry paste
Soy sauce, reduced-sodium (or use Bragg)
Sweet soy sauce (Kepac Manis)
  (or use dark soy sauce & honey)
3 cans tomato pasta sauce, Spicy Onion & Garlic
  (24 fl oz or 680 mL each)
Pizza sauce (1/2 cup)
1 can tomato soup (10 fl oz or 284 mL)
Chicken broth, reduced-sodium (3/4 cup)
Artichoke hearts (from a can)
Olives, sliced (optional for Mediterranean Pizza)
Sundried tomatoes (6-8) (in a jar)
Salad dressing, randch, light, or your favorite
  (choose a lower sodium brand)

■ FROZEN FOODS

Sweet potato fries (1 lb or 450 g) (or regular fries)
Baby peas (3 cups) (or use leftover veggies)

■ BAKERY

2 thin-crust pizza crusts (12")
Naan bread (optional for Butter Chicken)

■ OTHER

Paper towels

Custom Eat Sheet™

RECIPE NAME   Page

_____
_____
_____
_____
_____

■ MEATS

■ DAIRY

■ PRODUCE

■ DRY ESSENTIALS

■ SPICES

■ BAKING GOODS

■ HELPERS

■ FROZEN FOODS

■ BAKERY

■ OTHER

▦ MEATS

10-12 chicken thighs, boneless, skinless
 (1 3/4 lbs or 800 g)
16-20 chicken filets, boneless, skinless
 (1 1/2 lbs or 675 g)
 or chicken breasts cut into strips
Ground beef, extra-lean (1 lb or 450 g)
Bacon, fully cooked, reduced-sodium, 8 strips

▦ DAIRY

Eggs (3)
Butter
Milk 1% milk fat (1 1/4 cups)
Cream 10% milk fat (1/2 cup)
Sour cream, light (1/2 cup) for 2 meals
Cottage cheese, 1% fat (2 cups)
Sharp cheddar cheese, light, grated (1/2 cup)
Mozzarella cheese, part-skim, shredded (2 cups)
Parmesan cheese, light, grated (1 cup) for 2 meals

▦ PRODUCE

Cherry or grape tomatoes (12)
Broccoli florets, 2-3 heads (1 lb or 450 g)
Cauliflower (1 /4 head)
Celery ribs (2)
English cucumber (1/2)
Red bell pepper (1/2)
Baby carrots (2 cups)
Onion
Red onion (1/8)
Green onions (2-3)
Baby spinach, prewashed (6 oz or 170 g)

▦ DRY ESSENTIALS

Basmati or white rice (1 1/2 cups)
Fettuccini pasta (3/4 lb or 340 g)
Corn flake crumbs (1 cup)

▦ SPICES

Bay leaves
Blackened cajun spice (optional to replace pepper)
Curry powder
Garlic and herb seasoning, salt-free
Hot chili flakes (optional)
Italian seasoning
Lemon pepper
Onion flakes
Original, all purpose seasoning, salt-free
Pepper
Table blend seasoning, salt-free

▦ BAKING GOODS

Canola oil
Olive oil, extra-virgin
Balsamic vinegar (for dipping focaccia bread)
Matchstick almonds (1/4 cup) for 2 meals

▦ HELPERS

1 can Italian or chili stewed tomatoes
 (14 fl oz or 400 mL)
Reserved tomato pasta sauce (7 cups)
 from Spaghetti dinner, page 68
 or purchase canned (56 fl oz or 1750 mL) for 2 meals
1 can consommé (10 fl oz or 284 g)
Dijon mustard
Plum sauce
 (optional for Chicken Fingers) *I like VH brand.*
Salad dressing, fruit vinaigrette, light, or your favorite
 choose a lower sodium brand
Mayonnaise, light
Soy sauce, reduced-sodium
Sambal Oelek (crushed chili paste)
Liquid honey

▦ FROZEN FOODS

Green or yellow whole beans (1 lb or 450 g)
Mixed veggies (3 cups)
Blueberries, wild (1/4 cup)

▦ BAKERY

French bread, crusty loaf
Buns or focaccia bread (optional for Soup)
Focaccia bread, herbed (for Chicken Fingers dinner)

▦ OTHER

Parchment paper (important)
Waxed paper

Custom Eat Sheet™

RECIPE NAME   Page

_____

_____

_____

_____

_____

■ MEATS

■ DAIRY

■ PRODUCE

■ DRY ESSENTIALS

■ SPICES

■ BAKING GOODS

■ HELPERS

■ FROZEN FOODS

■ BAKERY

■ OTHER

RECIPE NAME	PAGE

■ MEATS

Chicken thighs, boneless, skinless (10-12)
  (1 3/4 lbs or 800 g)
Chicken breasts, boneless, skinless (3)
  (1 lb or 450 g)
Sirloin steak, lean, boneless (450 g)
  (can use flank steak or chicken breast for Fajitas)
Ground beef, extra-lean (2 lbs or 900 g)
  (or ground turkey)
Pork ribs, back or side, lean (2 1/2 lbs or 1125 g)

■ DAIRY

Eggs (2)
Milk, 1% milk fat (2 1/2 cups) for 2 meals
Sour cream, fat-free or light
  (1/2 cup + optional for Fajitas)
Cheddar cheese, light, shredded (2 cups)
  for 2 meals
Parmesan cheese, light, grated
  (optional for Tortellini)
Cheese tortellini (12 oz or 350 g) *Tricolor is nice.*

■ PRODUCE

Fresh garlic (from a jar) or use cloves
Veggies for Veggies & Dip (1 lb or 450 g)
  (e.g. celery, cauliflower, baby carrots, broccoli,
  or use precut veggies)
Broccoli florets, 2-3 heads (1 lb or 450 g)
Celery (1 rib)
Zucchini, small
Tomato, Roma (4)
Green bell pepper (2) for 2 meals
Red bell pepper (2) for 2 meals
Mushrooms (15) for 2 meals
Romaine lettuce, 1 head or bag (6 oz or 175 g)
  for 2 meals
Green onion (2)
Onion (2) for 3 meals
Red onion, small, or use regular onion
Baby potatoes, red (20)

■ OTHER

Aluminum foil
Paper towel

■ SPICES

Chili powder
Cinnamon, ground
Coriander
Cumin, ground
Onion flakes
Garlic & herb seasoning, salt-free
Garlic powder
Hot chili flakes (optional)
Original, all purpose seasoning, salt-free
Pepper
Sesame seeds, toasted (optional for Mole Chicken)

■ BAKING GOODS

Cooking spray
Canola oil
Olive oil, extra-virgin
Red wine vinegar

■ HELPERS

Basil pesto
Southwest BBQ sauce (1/4 cup) (or make own, page 94)
Honey-garlic sauce (12 oz or 341 mL)
  I like VH brand. (or make your own, see Ribs)
Worcestershire sauce
Salsa, chunky (mild, medium or hot) (2 1/2 cups)
  for 3 meals
Hot pepper relish, or chopped up jalapenos
  (optional for Meatloaf)
Mayonnaise, light
Salad dressing, ranch, light, or your favorite
  (choose a lower sodium brand)
Chicken broth, reduced-sodium
  (18 fl oz or 500 mL) for 2 meals
1 can mushroom soup, reduced-sodium
  (10 fl oz or 284 mL)
Peanut butter, light (or use almond butter)
Chocolate syrup *I use Quick*

■ DRY ESSENTIALS

Basmati or white rice (1 1/2 cups)

■ FROZEN FOODS

Stir-fry mixed vegetables (4 cups) (or use fresh)

■ BAKERY

Breadcrumbs (1 1/2 cups)
Bread rolls (6) (optional for Honey-Garlic Ribs)
Tortillas, soft (6) flour, multigrain or corn, 10"
  (choose a lower sodium brand)

Custom Eat Sheet™

RECIPE NAME   Page

_____

_____

_____

_____

_____

■ MEATS

■ DAIRY

■ PRODUCE

■ DRY ESSENTIALS

■ SPICES

■ BAKING GOODS

■ HELPERS

■ FROZEN FOODS

■ BAKERY

■ OTHER

■ MEATS

Chicken breasts (3), boneless, skinless (1 lb or 450 g)
Ground beef, extra-lean (1 1/2 lbs or 675 g)
Ground turkey (1 lb or 450 g)
Pork loin chops, 1/2" thick, boneless, trimmed (4)
Roaster chicken, deli cooked (3 cups cut chicken)

■ DAIRY

Butter
Milk, 1% milk fat
Cottage cheese, 1% milk fat (1 cup)
Mozzarella cheese, part-skim, shredded (1 cup)
Parmesan cheese, light, grated

■ PRODUCE

Fresh garlic (from a jar)
Celery ribs (2)
Broccoli florets, 2-3 heads (1 lb or 450 g)
Green bell pepper (2) 1 optional for Curied Chicken
Red bell pepper (1) for 2 meals
Mushrooms (17) for 2 meals
Cucumber, English or field
Baby carrots (1 cup)
Baby potatoes (20) or 4 large, thin skin
Onion, small
Green onions (2)
Spinach, 1 bag (6 oz or 175 g)

■ DRY ESSENTIALS

Basmati or white rice (1 1/4 cups)
Manicotti noodles (8 oz or 250 g)
Spaghetti pasta (12 oz or 340 g)
Panko flakes or cornflake crumbs
  (found near coating mixes)

■ OTHER

Aluminum foil
Paper towel

■ SPICES

Basil, dried
Cayenne pepper
Curry powder
Italian seasoning
Original, all purpose seasoning, salt-free
Pepper
Poultry seasoning
Table blend seasoning, salt-free

■ BAKING GOODS

Brown sugar
Cornstarch
Dry brown gravy mix (I like Bisto)
Olive oil, extra-virgin
Cooking spray
Vinegar
Balsamic vinegar
Cashews (1/4 cup) optional for Salad

■ HELPERS

Dijon mustard
Salad dressing, light, fruit vinaigrette or your favorite
  (choose a lower sodium brand)
Soy sauce, reduced-sodium
Cranberry sauce, whole berry (1/2 cup)
1 can beef broth, reduced-sodium
  (10 fl oz or 284 mL)
2 cans cream of mushroom soup, reduced-sodium
  (10 fl oz or 284 mL each) for 2 meals
1 can consommé soup (10 fl oz or 284 mL)
1 can pineapple chunks, unsweetened
  (20 oz or 540 mL)
1 can tomato pasta sauce
  choose a lower sodium brand (24 oz or 680 mL)
Basil pesto (1/4 cup) (found near pasta sauces)

■ FROZEN FOODS

Pea pods (10 oz or 300 g)
Baby peas (4 cups) for 2 meals

■ BAKERY

Multigrain bread, 1 loaf sliced (18 slices)

171

Custom Eat Sheet™

RECIPE NAME   Page

_____

_____

_____

_____

_____

■ MEATS

■ DAIRY

■ PRODUCE

■ DRY ESSENTIALS

■ SPICES

■ BAKING GOODS

■ HELPERS

■ FROZEN FOODS

■ BAKERY

■ OTHER

■ MEATS

Chicken breasts w/ skin, bone in (4)
  (1 3/4 lb or 800 g)
Chicken cutlets (1 1/3 lb or 600 g)
Ground beef, extra-lean
  (2 1/2 lb or 1125 g) for 2 meals
Bacon bits (optional for Spinach Salad)

■ DAIRY

Butter
Egg (1)
Cottage cheese, 1% (1/2 cup)
Feta cheese, light, crumbled (1/3 cup)
Ricotta cheese (1 cup)
Parmesan cheese, light grated (1/4 cup)
Mozzarella cheese, part-skim, shredded (1/2 cup)
Cambozola cheese or cream cheese (for Burgers)

■ PRODUCE

Fresh ginger (from a jar)
Fresh garlic (from a jar)
Baby carrots (3 cups) for 2 meals
Celery ribs (2)
Asparagus spears (20)
Green onions (1 bunch)
Cauliflower (for Italian Tossed Veggies)
Red bell pepper
Cucumber, English
Onion, small or onion flakes (for Tangy Meatlballs)
Red onion
Shallot
Lettuce (2 cups for Burgers)
Romaine lettuce, 1 bag (6 oz or 170 g)
Tomatoes (2)
Cherry tomatoes (8-12)
Baby potatoes (20) or 4 large potatoes
Snap peas (5 cups) for 3 meals
Zucchini, small
Cilantro (optional for Ginger Beef)

■ BAKERY

Hamburger buns, multigrain (6)

■ SPICES

Cayenne or chipotle pepper
  (optional for Burger coating)
Celery salt
Original, all purpose seasoning, salt-free
Paprika
Hot chili flakes
Pepper

■ BAKING GOODS

Canola oil
Olive oil, extra-virgin
Sesame oil
Vinegar
Rice vinegar
Brown sugar

■ HELPERS

Apricot jam (or use fig or peach jam)
Basil pesto (found near pasta sauces)
1 can tomato-basil pasta sauce (24 fl oz or 680 mL)
  choose a lower sodium brand
1 can tomato paste (5 1/2 fl oz or 156 mL)
  choose a lower sodium brand
Mayonnaise, light
Worcestershire sauce
Soy sauce, reduced-sodium
Sweet chili sauce (1/4 cup)
Red pepper jelly (or use apple jelly) (for Burgers)
  found near gourmet condiments
Caesar salad dressing, light (for Caesar Salad & for Dip)
  or you can use ranch
Italian dressing, light

■ FROZEN FOODS

Chopped spinach (3 1/2 oz or 100 g)

■ OTHER

Waxed paper
Parchment paper
Paper towel
Large freezer bag

■ DRY ESSENTIALS

Basmati or white rice (1 1/2 cups)
Croutons (optional for Spinach Salad)
Cornflake crumbs (found near coating mixes)
Pasta shells, 24 large (8 oz or 225 g)
  (also named conchiglioni rigati)
Egg noodles, broad (3/4 lb or 340 g)

Custom Eat Sheet™

RECIPE NAME   Page

_____

_____

_____

_____

_____

■ MEATS

■ DAIRY

■ PRODUCE

■ DRY ESSENTIALS

■ SPICES

■ BAKING GOODS

■ HELPERS

■ FROZEN FOODS

■ BAKERY

■ OTHER

174

RECIPE NAME

■ MEATS

Ground beef, extra-lean (1 lb or 450 g)
Chicken thighs, boneless, skinless (10-12)
  (1 3/4 lb or 800 g)
Chicken breasts, boneless, skinless (3) (1 lb or 450 g)
Sirloin or round roast, boneless, trimmed
  (2-3 lbs or 900-1350 g) Can double for leftovers.

■ DAIRY

Butter
Cheddar cheese, light, shredded (1/2 cup)
Parmesan cheese, light, grated
Vanilla yogurt, low-fat (1/2 cup)
Spinach and cheese ravioli (3/4 lb or 350 g)

■ PRODUCE

Broccoli florets, 2-3 heads (1 lb or 450 g)
Baby carrots (1 lb or 450 g)
Onion, small
Zucchini, small
Green bell pepper (1/2)
Red bell pepper (1/2)
Mushrooms (10)
Baby potatoes (20) (or 4 large potatoes)
Red grapes (1 1/2 cups)
Mandarins (3)

■ BAKERY

Hamburger buns, whole wheat (4-6)

■ DRY ESSENTIALS

Basmati or white rice (1 1/2 cups)
  (or mixed rice - *I like Canoe brand*)
Spaghettini pasta (3/4 lb or 340 g)

■ SPICES

Basil leaves
Chili powder
Cumin, ground
Curry powder
Garlic and herb seasoning, salt-free
Lemon pepper
Onion flakes
Original all purpose seasoning, salt-free

■ BAKING GOODS

Canola oil
Olive oil, extra-virgin
Balsamic vinegar
Cornstrach
Dry brown gravy mix (*I like Bisto*)

■ HELPERS

1 can fruit salad, unsweetened (14 fl oz or 398 mL)
Ketchup
Mustard, prepared
Honey, liquid
Maple syrup
Worcestershire sauce
Honey-garlic sauce (*I like VH*)
Soy sauce, reduced-sodium
Teriyaki sauce
Chicken broth, reduced-sodium (1 1/2 cups)
  (for 2 meals)
1 can beef broth, reduced-sodium (10 fl oz or 284 mL)
1 can cream of asparagus soup (10 fl oz or 284 mL)
Salsa (1 cup) for 2 meals
Basil pesto

■ FROZEN FOODS

Green or yellow whole beans (1 lb or 450 g)

■ OTHER

Aluminum foil

Custom Eat Sheet™

RECIPE NAME   Page

_____

_____

_____

_____

_____

◼ MEATS

◼ DAIRY

◼ PRODUCE

◼ DRY ESSENTIALS

◼ SPICES

◼ BAKING GOODS

◼ HELPERS

◼ FROZEN FOODS

◼ BAKERY

◼ OTHER

RECIPE NAME	PAGE

■ MEATS

Chicken breasts, boneless, skinless (9)
  (3 1/4 lbs or 1.5 kg) for 3 meals
  (or replace 4 breasts with 10 thighs for Parmesan)
Shrimp, large, cooked, peeled and deveined
  (1 lb or 450 g) (or use chicken)
Ground beef, extra-lean (1 1/2 lbs or 675 g)

■ DAIRY

Butter
Milk, 1% milk fat (2 1/2 cups) for 2 meals
Sour cream, fat-free or light
Mozzarella cheese, part-skim, shredded (2 1/2 cups)
  for 2 meals
Parmesan cheese, light, grated (1 cup) for 2 meals

■ PRODUCE

Fresh garlic (from a jar)
Baby carrots (3 cups) for 2 meals
Asparagus spears (20) (1 lb or 450 g)
Celery ribs (6) for 2 meals
Broccoli florets (1 lb or 450 g) for 2 meals
  (+ 3/4 lb or 340 g if not using frozen in Stew)
Cauliflower (1/4 head) for Fresh Veggies
Onion (2) for 2 meals
Cucumber, English
Green onion (optional for BBQ Pizza)
Red onion (1/8) (optional for Chicken Parmesan)
Green bell pepper (1/2)
Red bell pepper (1 1/2) for 2 meals
Mushrooms (17) for 2 meals
Tomato (optional for BBQ Pizza)
Grape tomatoes (1 cup) (for Italian Veggies)
Potatoes, thin skin, large (4) (2 lbs or 900 g)
  New Yukon potatoes don't need to be peeled.
Romaine lettuce leaves (2 leaves)
  or any other lettuce (topping for BBQ Pizza)

■ DRY ESSENTIALS

Basmati or white rice (1 1/2 cups)
Penne pasta (3 cups)
Linguini pasta (12 oz or 340 g)

■ SPICES

Basil leaves
Chili powder
Chipotle seasoning
Cumin, ground
Dill, dried
Garlic and herb seasoning, salt-free
Hot chili flakes (optional for Creamy Pesto Shrimp)
Lemon pepper
Onion flakes
Parsley, dried
Pepper
Table blend seasoning, salt-free

■ BAKING GOODS

Cooking spray
Canola oil
Olive oil, extra-virgin
Balsamic vinegar
Flour

■ HELPERS

Salsa, chunky (mild, medium or hot) (1/2 cup)
Southwest BBQ sauce (1 Tbsp for BBQ Pizza)
Worcestershire sauce
Salad dressing, ranch, light (optional for Fresh Veggies)
Italian dressing, light
1 can Italian stewed tomatoes (19 fl oz or 540 mL)
1 can cream of chicken soup, reduced-sodium
  (10 fl oz or 284 mL)
1 can tomato pasta sauce (24 fl oz or 680 mL)
  choose a lower sodium brand
Basil pesto

■ FROZEN FOODS

Corn (1 cup) (I like Peaches & Cream style)
Baby carrots (1/2 lb or 225 g)
Broccoli florets (3/4 lb or 340 g)
  (can use fresh broccoli for Stew)

■ BAKERY

Pizza base, thin crust 12" (1/2 lb or 225 g)

■ OTHER

Aluminum foil
Paper towel

Conversion Charts

Liquid Measure		Dry Measures	Approx	Measuring	Approx	Exact
1 oz	30 ml	1 oz	30 g	1/4 tsp	1.2 ml	
2 oz	60 ml	4 oz (1/4 lb)	125 g	1/2 tsp	2.4 ml	
3 oz	100 ml	8 oz (1/2 lb)	250 g	1 tsp	5 ml	(4.7)
4 oz	125 ml	12 oz (3/4 lb)	375 g	1 Tbsp (3 tsp)	15 ml	(14.2)
5 oz	150 ml	16 oz (1 lb)	500 g	1/4 cup (4 Tbsp)	55 ml	(56.8)
6 oz	190 ml	32 oz (2 lbs)	1 kg	1/3 cup	75 ml	(75.6)
8 oz	250 ml	**Buying Meat or Produce**		1/2 cup	125 ml	(113.7)
10 oz (1/2 pint)	300 ml	1/2 lb	225 g	2/3 cup	150 ml	(151.2)
16 oz (1/2 litre)	500 ml	1 lb	450 g	3/4 cup	175 ml	(170)
20 oz (1 pint)	600 ml	1 1/2 lbs	675 g	1 cup	250 ml	(227.3)
1 3/4 pints (1 litre)	1000 ml	2 lbs	900 g	4 1/2 cups	1 litre (L)	(1022.9)
		2 1/2 lbs	1125 g			
		3 lbs	1350 g			

Conversion Charts

Oven Temperatures				Can	Jar	%	If You Eat...	Your Daily Fat Intake Should Be
F	C	F	C	4.5 oz	127 ml		1500 calories	50 grams
175 - 80		350 - 175		8 oz	227 ml	30%	2000 calories	67 grams
200 - 95		375 - 190		10 oz	284 ml	30%	2500 calories	83 grams
225 - 110		400 - 205	mod hot	12 oz	341 ml		3000 calories	100 grams
250 - 120		425 - 220		14 oz	398 ml		1500 calories	42 grams
275 - 140		450 - 230	hot	19 oz	540 ml	25%	2000 calories	56 grams
300 - 150		475 - 240		24.5 oz	700 ml	25%	2500 calories	69 grams
325 - 160		500 - 260	very hot				3000 calories	83 grams
							1500 calories	33 grams
						20%	2000 calories	44 grams
						20%	2500 calories	56 grams
							3000 calories	67 grams

RECIPE NAME	PAGE

■ MEATS
Ground beef, extra-lean (3 lbs or 900 g) for 2 meals
Chicken breasts, boneless, skinless (7)
  (2 1/3 lbs or 1 kg) for 2 meals
Shrimp (1 cup) cooked, deveined (optional for Quiche)

■ DAIRY
Butter
Milk, 1% milk fat (1 cup) for 2 meals
Cream 10% milk fat (1/4 cup)
Eggs, large (4)
Parmesan cheese, light, grated (optional for Taco Pasta)
Gruyere cheese (1/4 cup) (can replace with Parmesan)
Mozzarella, part-skim, shredded (1/4 cup)
Cheddar cheese, light (1/2 cup) can use grated

■ PRODUCE
Fresh ginger (from a jar) or use ground
Fresh garlic (from a jar)
Carrots, large (2)
Cucumber, English (1/2)
Broccoli floret (1 1/4 lbs or 560 g) for 2 meals
Green leaf lettuce (1/4 head) (or bagged lettuce)
  for Thai Wraps
Red bell pepper (1 1/4) for 2 meals
Mushrooms (14) for 2 meals
Baby spinach, bag (6 oz or 170 g)
Bean sprouts (1/2 lb or 225 g) (optional for Thai Wraps)
Potatoes, large, thin skin (4) or 8 medium (2 lbs or 900 g)
Onion (1 1/4) for 2 meals
Onion, red (1/8) for Spinach Salad
Zucchini, small (2-3)
Roma tomato (optional for Quiche)

■ DRY ESSENTIALS
Basmati or white rice (1 1/2 cups)
Rice stick or vermicelli noodles (1/4 lb or 113 g)
Pasta, bow tie (3 cups)

■ SPICES
Chili powder
Cumin, ground
Garlic and herb seasoning, salt-free
Ginger, ground
Hot chili flakes (optional for Taco Pasta)
Original all purpose seasoning, salt-free
Pepper
Turmeric

■ BAKING GOODS
Cooking spray
Canola oil
Olive oil, extra-virgin
Sesame oil
Rice vinegar (1 Tbsp)
Matchstick almonds (for Spinach Salad)
Biscuit mix (*I like Bisquick*)
Brown sugar

■ HELPERS
Lime juice (for 2 meals)
Peanut butter, light (for Thai Wraps)
Ketchup
Soy sauce, reduced-sodium
Sweet Thai chili sauce (for 2 meals)
Worcestershire sauce
Catalina salad dressing, low-fat (optional if replacing
sweet Thai Chili sauce in Thai Wrap sauce)
Fruit vinaigrette, light (or your favorite dressing)
1 can beef broth, reduced-sodium (10 fl oz or 284 mL)
1 can cream style corn (14 fl oz or 398 mL)
1 can tomato pasta sauce (24 fl oz or 680 mL)
  (choose a lower sodium brand)

■ FROZEN FOODS
Corn, Peaches & Cream style (1 cup)
Peas (4 cups) (1 1/3 lbs or 600 g)
Wild blueberries (1/2 cup) for Spinach Salad

■ BAKERY
Tortillas, soft (6) whole wheat or flour, 10"
  (choose a lower sodium brand)

■ OTHER
Paper towel

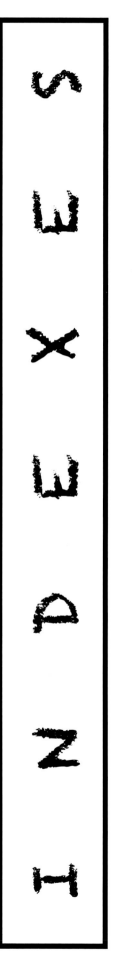

Main Component

beef, chicken, pork, seafood, vegetarian

'cause you have an idea
of what you'd like

Prep Code

by color
for when timing is everything

Fat Content

from lowest to highest

'cause your health requires you
to watch your fat intake

Index by Main Component

Index By Main Component

Make It Vegetarian!

(see *About the Recipes* pages for details)

Index By Prep Code

Index By Fat Content

Adjusting Nutritional Data
To Your Specific Needs

Most of the recipes in Eating Forward™ provide 4-6 servings.

If you have 4 adults in your home with very healthy appetites the meal will probably serve 4 (when we write Serves 4-6). Sometimes someone gets a left-over lunch the next day!

If you have younger children the recipe will probably serve 6 (when we write Serves 4-6).

When a range is given for the number of servings a meal makes, the higher number is used.

(i.e. When a meal says 4-6 servings, the nutritional data assumes you are dividing every component of the entire meal into 6 portions. The nutritional data is for one portion of each component. This also applies to the food exchange and food group data.)

Use the formula below to adjust the nutritional data when *we* write "Serves 4-6" and for *your* family it serves 4.

Adjusting Data when a Meal Serves 4 instead of 6

of g fat x 1.5 = # of g fat

i.e. 12 g fat x 1.5 = 18 g fat

(12 g fat per serving for 6 servings) = (18 g fat per serving for 4 servings)

This formula works for all our nutritional data.

Weights and Measures

- Imperial and Metric conversions are approximate only.
- When more than one unit of measure is provided, nutritional data is calculated using the first named.
- When a range is given for a measure, the first given is used to calculate nutritional data.
- When a choice of two ingredients are listed (i.e. chicken or pork), the first is used for nutritional data.
- Ingredients listed as "optional" are not included in nutritional data.
- Buns are 1 1/2 oz (or 45 g).
- **Our meals most often adhere to the following guidelines for the complete dinner:**
  Calories: 350-500 calories/serving; **Fat**: less than 25 g/serving; **Carbohydrates**: 30-70 g/serving; **Protein**: 25-35 g/serving; **Sodium**: less than 1000 mg/serving
  Calories from fat should not exceed 30% of your total caloric intake each day.

Diabetic Food Choices and Food Exchanges

Canada's Choices and America's Exchanges are included for each meal in our book.

Nutritional data, including food choices and exchanges, are calculated for the entire meal (per serving).

Visit **www.diabetes.ca** for information and resources from the **Canadian Diabetes Association**'s website.

Visit **www.diabetes.org** for the exchange list, the pyramid, information, and resources from the **American Diabetes Association**'s website.

Our Team

God - no picture on file
God - you did it again! You knew all along that teens could help their families get back to the dinner table, despite everyone's crazy busy schedule! Thank you, once again, for believing in me and trusting that I will serve well! I don't know what I would do if you were not part of our team!

Captain - Ron Richard
It seems like yesterday, yet forever ago, when Ron convinced me to follow my passion and help families get back to the dinner table! What I didn't realize was that as a result of his support he too would find his passion---running every aspect of our business. Within one year of Life's on Fire's release, Ron left teaching and has been Captain of our team ever since! Whether he's coordinating a new book project, being chief financial officer or managing me he's my very special boss! We work together every single day and I can honestly say I love you more today than ever before---and you're pretty cute too! Ron is the co-owner of our company.
Cooking for the Rushed Inc.   info@cookingfortherushed.com

Food Photography - Lisa Fryklund
Lisa is with us once again and once again we are astounded with how she manages to make real food (not food styled) look so great! She has become a trusted member of our team and a dear friend! We love you Lis! Lisa is a photographer and an award winning cinematographer with a wide range of experience. She has travelled the world filming for Discovery, TLC, CBC, ABC, History, CMT, HGTV and National Geographic. Lisa Fryklund is the owner of her own company.
Fryklund Cinematography   www.fryklund.com

Food Photography - Ian Grant
Photo credits for pages: 47, 49, 55, 57, 67, 81, 93, 103, 109, 127, 135, 145

Illustrations - Hermann Brandt - Hermann is an amazing artist and illustrator! He studied art at the Pretoria Technicon Arts School in South Africa and is the owner of his own company.
Clear Air Art Studio   http://clearairartstudio.blogspot.com

Illustrations - Lorna Bennett - We just had to incorporate some of Lorna's classics!
Lorna Bennet Illustration   http://www.lornabennett.net

Our Team

Graphic Design and Illustrations - James Simon

James is new to our team this year. We can't say enough about how multi talented this guy is! He and Ron were in charge of the entire production of *Anyone Can Cook Dinner*. In addition to being the lead graphic designer on the project, he did some of the illustrations as well! When he's not wielding his superhero talents at the computer, he's film editing or creating comic books! James was the lead video editor and graphics coordinator for the 2002 World Arnold games, has edited hundreds of commercials and taught editing at The Toronto Film School. James is owner of his own company Afrovince.com and now we are honored to be part of his hero's journey! I almost forgot... he really likes peanut butter!

Everything by Afrovince   www.afrovince.com

Cover Photography, Teen Shots and Sandi's Photos - Robert Nowell

Robert Nowell is new to our team as well. After moving to St. Catharines, and away from all our old familiar gang, we were a little nervous when we needed some extra photos and a cover shot. Rob has been an absolute treat to work with! He says, "When I hold a camera, everything just clicks"! He has done countless magazine covers and is the most amazing portrait photographer. Rob is the owner of his own company Robert Nowell Photographer located in St. Catharine's, Ontario, Canada.

Robert Nowell Photographer   www.robertnowellphoto.com

Dietitian, Diabetes Consultant - Sandra Burgess B.A.Sc., R.D., C.D.E.

Sandra joins us once again to convert all our nutritional data to U.S. and Canadian diabetes food exchange and food group values. She has been an invaluable member of our team and we feel very blessed to have her on board once again! Sandra is an avid volunteer with the Canadian Diabetes Association, Inn from the Cold Society and the very famous Calgary Stampede. She is a registered dietitian and certified diabetes educator with over 30 years of experience.

Editing - The Girls (Sylvia, Catherine, Melissa, Carm, Caroline and Jacqueline)

Friends have always been a special part of our team! Every book has had a customary "friend edit". The girls come over and pick the book apart, piece-by-piece! We chat, we laugh, we share stories and yes, we even edit! We banter about which words are proper or not and where punctuation should be or shouldn't be! It's like the book's final blessing! I was pretty sad this time around, not being home with my friends, so likely no "friend edit". Buuut, as the saying goes, when one door closes another opens.
Thank you, thank you, thank you for being this book's final blessing!

A Note from Sandi

Our young adults need us to get out of their way and let them cook!

When the kids were growing up, our fridge seemed to disappear behind all the pictures, school announcements and newspaper clippings. Ooooh yes, I remember one newspaper article in particular… a silhouette of three teens taking a short-cut home on the train trestle over the river. There were big bold letters underneath that read, "Dork #1, #2 and #3". I was soooo proud that a teen of mine posted this up for all to see! I bragged to my friend how much common sense my teens had as I pointed to the picture and the words! Then… THEN in horror I realized the handwriting was Dougie's and Dork #1 was Candice!!! (That's a whole different POT of tea story.)

All grown up!

Amidst the clutter, which was randomly held up by an assortment of mismatched magnets (ranging from bought ones with favorite sayings like, "YOU CAN'T SCARE ME, I HAVE KIDS" to tooth shaped ones with our dentist's telephone number… in case of a dental emergency I guess!) were three items that were always cladding the fridge. The infamous Maintenance List, the Snack White Board and that week's Eat Sheet. Each meal had a name beside it. I remember our teens insinuating, from time to time, that the world would be appalled if it knew their famous, meal planning, mom made them cook!!! For the most part though, you could tell they actually enjoyed it (except for Paige)!

On the topic of food, my teens were like everyone else's. They would look deeeep into the stuffed pantry…emerging with glazed over eyes, whining, "theere's noooothing to eeeat! Some liked to cook and others not so much!

Dan warned that he was going to drink soda pop and eat boxed mac and cheese for life, after he moved out! Paige swore she would NEVER, EVER, EVER cook! Jeffy thought being forced to cook on his meal night was some sort of child abuse. Candice and Nikki loved to cook but mostly loved to bake (even when their brownies looked more like soup than brownies)! We have witnesses! Dougie got into cooking so much that he even worked with us to get our first book out and then managed two different restaurants. (He now owns a successful construction company-go figure)! Courtney was always more fascinated with the science of food than cooking itself, but took on each dinner challenge with enthusiasm and humor! She was the house comedian! I guess being the youngest of seven kids, it was either laugh or cry. Don't worry, honey, I won't divulge what you'd repeat, as you stood up on your chair, if you weren't given a chance to speak! Your secret's safe with me! (Aaand six siblings - good luck!)

A Note from Sandi

Aly & Me (Grandma)

So here's the thing… I have seven kids, (with seven different personalities) aaand they all cook!

Dan, my mac and cheese guy, just served us a Thai dish he came up with himself. He wants me to put it in our next book. He finally had to admit mac and cheese and soda pop didn't make him feel so hot in the long term! Candice is an amazing cook (and still loves to bake, quite successfully now - and swears the brownies weren't that bad!) Like I said, I have witnesses! Nikki's an amazing cook too and also claims the brownies weren't that bad! (I HAVE WITNESSES!)

Not only does Jeffy like to cook, he raves about his cooking appliances, knives aaaand regularly likes to teach me things, like how to properly brush a mushroom! Uhuh - it's true! Courtney still has a fascination with the science of food and is an amazing cook as well (and can still have us all belly laughing at the drop of a hat!) …Aaand Paige; She cooks a lot... shhhhh don't tell anyone!

Dougie not only cooks, he is now getting our granddaughter, Aly, to cook. Aly is very proud of the things she knows how to do on her own (and can even roll a spring roll and use chop sticks better than I can)!

Can you just imagine what would happen if teens everywhere understood that cooking is freedom and independence? Can you imagine what would happen if they stood up for their right to great health? They can change everything! And they will! I believe if parents all across North America let this happen, it can be a reality that will benefit us all!!!

A few years back Sarah Woodruff, PhD CEP (University of Windsor) and I spoke to a large group of dietitians and nutritionists. The topic revolved around understanding teen behavior and how it relates to eating dinner at home. She presented research facts and I presented family realities (as seen through the eyes of a meal planner)! After the conference Sarah and I made a pact that we were going to figure out how to work together. (Believe me this is not as easy as you may think considering she is in the public sector and I am in the private sector.) We decided our company would work on the school presentations and workbooks, and her team would cover anything that was connected to the research. I would try and get corporations to fork over a little cash to fund the school projects and she would try and get the government to support her team's research. Anything great takes time! We soft launched Kinect-Ed (teen chefs in charge) and even we couldn't have imagined the astounding results! Way to Go Teens of Windsor-Essex! Say a prayer for us as we approach round two in 2012/13!

If you are a corporation interested in hearing more about changing the health of our country, through our teens, we'd love to hear from you!

189

Our Amazing Test Families...

I have always believed, since our first book *Life's on Fire - Cooking for the Rushed*, that families needed to test the meal recipe in their own kitchens. Sure it can start in a test kitchen, but remember, foodies love food and aren't testing it within a complex living situation! I will never forget how hard it was back in 1997-98! Getting families to test the meals for us was like pulling teeth! We would tell them we were testing for our meal planning and cookbook series, Cooking for the Rushed, and we needed real families in real time to do the meals! Most said they didn't have time! We would say, "That's the point, it will save you time"! We ended up begging families and little by little many agreed! Once they started, they wanted to test more weeks. They told their friends and there lay the foundation for our strict real life testing. Hundreds of thousands of families now use our books and are geting back to the dinner table! Hundreds of families, across North America ask us if they can be test families now! How blessed are we!

This time around the testing was very different. The families had to involve their kids' aged 10-20 in the cooking process (Whether they were Cooking Together/Apart™ or cooking together they did an amazing job)!

Here are the family names and their children who were involved in cooking!

The Beally family: Julie
The Blasken family: Jameson and Megan
The Bolduc family: Alexandre and Frederick
The Browne family: Micah
The Cargill family: Samuel
The Cannon Family: Conor and Graeme
The Currie family: Kennedy
The Dollar-Thompson family: Cameron and Madison
The Fears family: Tavio and Duncan
The Fraser family: Talia
The Grandquist family: Wyatt and Lauren
The Hall family: Clara
The Homeniuk family: Chris, Amanda, and Olivia
The Kiser family: Ted
The Kravitz-Kirsch family: Samantha and Adam

The Legedza family: Ashley
The Lescorbeau-Stokes family: Paige and Olivia
The Lujan family: Carson
The Moulin Family: Mary and Maddie
The Moussa family: Natalie
The Reid family: Justin and Quinten
The Richardson family: Maren
The Rieger family: Colin and Kyle
The Sipple family: Fiona
The Schiebel family: Meghan
The Stoutjesdyk family: Marielle
The Thom family: Sarah, Jessica and Michael
The Voldeng family: Jeremy and Miranda
The Verrier-Tittlemier family: Mathieu and Katlin
The Weir family: Julia and Erica

Here are a few of the comments from these up and coming amazing adults and their parents:

Maddie Moulin: "I want the chicken burger with hot pepper jelly for my birthday."

Samuel Cargill: " I have the confidence to cook dinner on my own."

Christina Hall: " Your books have been a part of our family since 1999. Now my daughter Clara is cooking (and even setting the table beautifully. We loved being a part of this!"

Mathieu Verrier: "Cooking is fun!"

Trina Verrier: "Mathieu is more likely to eat the food he hand prepares."

Wyatt Gandquist: "My favorite recipe is the BBQ Southwest Chicken pizza. I didn't even pick any veggies off and now I like green onions!"

Lauren Grandquist: "My favorite recipe was the meatloaf. I liked mixing it with my hands and squishing it between my fingers. Maybe my favorite was the ribs…I don't know-I liked them both a lot!"

Talia Young: "I didn't know I liked to cook until my mom made me do this! I love eating dinner together every night; it's my favorite part of the day! My mom and I get to talk and I have so much fun (I even forget to complain about the things I don't like)!"

Erica Rossi: "The Curried Chicken and Spaghetti rocks!" - **Patti Weir:** "This quote is from a really picky eater! We've made it twice since testing!"

Dale and Angela Voldeng: " Sandi, your books have changed the way we sit down to dinner. We actually sit down to dinner now! Shopping is a breeze, and I love planning my week, knowing what we'll have for dinner each night. I am so glad my sister introduced me to these books!"

My Books

What you can count on!
The same platform, so no matter what book you use you get the same benefits.

The platform for all books
Six times tested and retested by real families on the go in real life. Each meal takes no longer than 20 minutes to prepare, is color coded for speed, and follows basic balanced eating, rather than diet fads. Each portion is a proper serving size, is limited to approx 500 calories for the whole meal with a few exceptions and follows healthy guidelines on fat, carbs and sodium. You make each meal by starting at the top and working your way down, reading left to right, just as you would a book. Our trademark format means less confusion during weekday cooking. Clocks indicate prep time and we even tell you when dinner is ready. Color photos of real food with no photography tricks. Equipment lists and coinciding Eat Sheets™ (grocery lists) for each week so that you are ready for the grocery store.

What makes each book different?

The Healthy Family
Helps our readers sift through the mounds of health information in the most simplified and fun way possible! Packed with advice from Dr. Kelly Brett and Dr. George Lambrose as well as a big thumbs up from Dr. Gordon Matheson M.D. PhD. from Stanford University, this book took complex information on the energy balance between food and activity and made it all very easy to understand. It's a fun, informative and provocative read! *The Healthy Family* has 7 full weeks of nutritionally balanced dinners with corresponding Eat Sheets™.

The (Family) Dinner Fix
I understand that our readers are becoming more sophisticated, as families in North America adopt the many different cultural foods our beautiful countries have to offer. With this in mind, I've taken work-week favorites and created 10 weeks of amazing dinners with corresponding Eat Sheets™.

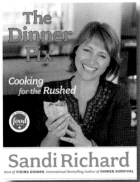

Dinner Survival
Takes a good look at the complexities of today's ever changing family. It offers tips and tricks to help you to get dinner to the table effortlessly. Everything from how to cook the perfect steak to "Why didn't my slow cooker recipe work?" Many of the meals were created for real families featured on my show *Fixing Dinner* on Food Network Canada, American Life and Discovery Asia. *Dinner Survival* has 10 weeks of amazing dinners with corresponding Eat Sheets™.

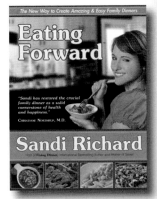

Eating Forward™
Sandi Richard's Eating Forward™ system is helping thousands of families enjoy dinner again. Eating Forward™, Sandi teaches you her system as never before, along with 10 more complete weeks of deliciously simple meals. Her common sense approach takes dinner off your mind. Save time, money, health and peace of mind!

DINNER CAN BE EASY!

Love dinner while improving your **health**, **budget** and **relationships**!

Sandi has an **Eating Forward**™ program for your organization, agency or corporation.

Why not **fundraise** with a program that brings families back to the dinner table...and promotes healthy eating on a budget?

Online free printable Eat Sheets™ for all books.

www.sandirichard.com

Eat Sheet™ Generator!

What is an Eat Sheet™ Generator?

It's software that allows you to choose dinners from any of Sandi's books, then print the grocery list.

Create your perfect dinner week!

1- Choose your favorite meals from any of Sandi's books
2- Print your own customized **Eat Sheet**™

www.sandirichard.com